"Full Belly Farm has been a perennial favorite of mine for the past nineteen years. When we opened Nopa in early 2006, our kitchen committed to a daily changing menu based on the most pristine organic produce I could get my hands on. Every Tuesday in Berkeley and Thursday in San Rafael, Full Belly Farm has helped make my wish a delicious reality. With an infectious ethos, obvious reverence for the land, multi-generational farming experience, and really, really hard work, Full Belly has set the bar for regenerative organic farms. Nopa loves Full Belly Farms!"

—**LAURENCE JOSSEL**, Chef/Owner, Nopa and Nopa Fish

"Full Belly Farm is a gold standard for what American farms could look like, supporting all the pillars of beneficial agriculture: biodiversity, polyculture, fair treatment of workers, recycling of nutrients . . . and production of fantastic food. With this cookbook, Amon and Jenna Muller—representatives of the third generation of Full Belly—demonstrate how their bounty can be best put to work in assembling beautiful meals."

—**MARK BITTMAN**, author of *How to Cook Everything*

For our beautiful children: Rowan, Arlo, and Hazel, who inspire us to continue to strive;

For our parents, for their support;

And for our crew, whose capable hands lift and carry Full Belly Farm. We couldn't do it without you.

FULL BELLY
FARM AND KITCHEN

Stories and recipes from a family farm

BY AMON & JENNA MULLER

Hardie Grant
NORTH AMERICA

TABLE OF CONTENTS

INTRODUCTION

As a kid growing up on a farm, I dreamed of fewer chores, more movie theaters, and miles of smooth pavement to rollerblade on. My parents, Paul Muller and Dru Rivers, moved to a crumbling dairy farm with an aging almond orchard when I was only six months old and built a thriving and abundant farm from the ground up, along with their business partners, Andrew Brait and Judith Redmond (who in many ways became like extra parents and role models for me). My siblings and I learned to crawl through vines of watermelons and run through tall stalks of sweet corn. In the early years, our parents would wake up hours before dawn to load up their old red pickup truck with sweet corn and their sleeping children and make the long trek to the Palo Alto farmers' market, where they started selling to reverent customers and a few restaurants, including the legendary Chez Panisse in Berkeley.

I took my idyllic childhood for granted and couldn't wait to get off the farm. I loathed the chores and hard work and imagined a simpler life in the city. After high school I took off for college and was sorely disappointed by city life. In my spare time I yearned for the outdoors and I became a rafting guide, learning to cook on the side of a river. I found myself reflecting on the experiences of the farm: The cooking lessons with my mom, who would routinely make lunch for all twenty of our crew, every day, for years. The hours in the mechanic's shop with my dad, developing a knack for fixing equipment and a hard work ethic. Above all, I carried a sense of what was in season and could pick out great produce with ease. I found that the experiences created around food, no matter where they are, are something that I enjoy immensely.

After graduating from college, I floated back to the farm for a summer and, without any real intention, wound up staying a year. I started to enjoy the hard work and sense of community, but I still wondered how I could make my mark. Around that time, I met my future wife and partner Jenna, a smart lawyer working at a prestigious law firm in San Francisco. I decided to give the city one last chance and worked at several restaurants, including Chez Panisse, Quince, and Coi. Talented chefs from those restaurants were longtime customers from the farmers' markets, and I got to see how they worked with our produce and transformed it for diners.

Ultimately, Jenna and I decided to return to the farm. Jenna wanted a lifestyle change in literal greener pastures, and I realized my real culinary mentor was always going to be the farm. We hatched a plan and hosted our first farm dinner in my parents' backyard in 2010. We rigged a small outdoor kitchen in the grassy peach orchard, set up an old picnic table that I had made as a teenager, and cooked a multicourse meal. We invited twenty friends to spend an evening on the farm and welcomed them to pitch a tent in the walnut grove.

After that we were hooked. Our farm dinners have grown with us over the past fourteen years. We built a commercial kitchen and event space in 2015, which now serves farm dinners, pizza nights, and even weddings. We got married ourselves and had three kids who are our best taste testers and harshest food critics. And we've become proud partners in the family business. As an adult today, I can see how my parents were early leaders in the organic movement, winning many awards and accolades. I hope to carry that same commitment to sustainability into the kitchen.

Consider this cookbook an invitation to dinner on the farm. That means simple recipes, because as farmers and parents, sometimes dinner is an afterthought at the end of a long, hot day. We feature seasonal ingredients, because when you live forty-five minutes from the nearest grocery store, or even if you don't but have a busy life, cooking has to get creative. These recipes are easy to scale up, because we're often cooking for a crew with large platters served family style. Plus we share a few preserving projects for jams and pickles, because we hate to let good food go to waste.

You're also in for a few family stories from life on the farm. In today's world that's obsessed with convenience, it can be easy to forget that every bunch of carrots that you pick up was harvested by a person. We hope this book fosters a sense of connection with the people who planted, cared for, and picked those carrots. If you're curious about where your food comes from, and might be interested in supporting local farms and food systems, please—take a seat at our family table. Don't mind the barefoot farm kids or overly friendly dogs. We're so glad you're here. ***Amon***

ABOUT FULL BELLY FARM

Full Belly Farm is a 400-acre certified organic farm in Northern California's Capay Valley. It is situated on the banks of Cache Creek, a tributary to the Sacramento River, on the ancestral ground of the Yocha Dehe Wintun Nation. Since 1985, we have farmed with a deep commitment to sustainability, using organic practices to build healthy soil, conserve water, and create a thriving, diverse ecosystem. We grow a wide variety of vegetables, fruits, nuts, herbs, and flowers year-round, and we also raise livestock—including chickens, sheep, goats, and cows—to help create a balanced, regenerative farm system.

Farming is a family effort. We, along with the other owners—Andrew Brait, Paul Muller, Dru Rivers, Rye Muller, and Hannah Muller—live and work here alongside our incredible crew of about eighty employees. Together, we care for the land using cover cropping, crop rotation, and minimal tillage, ensuring that every harvest supports the long-term health of our soil. We also believe that a farm should be a place of connection and community. Every year, we welcome thousands of visitors for farm tours, school visits, and hands-on events like our Hoes Down Harvest Festival, farm dinners, pizza nights, and weddings.

In 2011, we started the process of building the Full Belly Farm Kitchen, turning our love of cooking into a way to share the flavors of the farm year-round. What began as small backyard dinners has grown into a thriving kitchen producing value-added products, a beloved farm dinner series, and meals that showcase the best of each season. Our products are sold at three Bay Area farmer's markets, through our CSA program, and to retail, wholesale, and restaurant accounts.

Full Belly Farm has always been a place of experimentation—whether it's growing new melon varieties, crafting a fermented hot sauce, or finding creative ways to care for the land. At the heart of it all is our love for good food, healthy soil, and the community that makes it all possible.

LATE
SPRING
MIDSUMMER
EARLY
SPRING
EARLY
SUMMER
SPRING
FALL
MID-FALL
WINTER

ORDER HERE
PICKUP
ICE CREAM
ICE CREAM HERE

SPRING

EARLY SPRING

MID-SPRING

LATE SPRING

PRESERVING SPRING

SPRING

Spring encompasses wild swings in both mood and weather. In February, the almonds begin to bloom and all 150 of our baby lambs are born. It was spring, many years ago, when I first met Amon. I was working in San Francisco at a large law firm when I heard from my very oldest friend. She told me she was working at a farm about two hours from the city and that I should come for a visit. It was a rainy and wet day, and we walked out to the lambing barn. A rugged-looking young farmer approached with a smile on his face and a baby lamb in his arms. I was a goner.

Much of spring involves waiting. We wait for the lambs to be born. We wait for the tulips to bloom and pray that they will be ready in time for Valentine's Day. We wait for the ground to be dry enough to plant our summer crops. We wait for the first of the strawberries and mulberries, the first fruits to ripen after a long stretch with only oranges, and watch as the first tender shoots of asparagus make their way out of the ground. We wait and hope that the last frost doesn't take all of the almond and stone fruit blossoms. We wait for it to be warm enough for the bees to start flying and pollinating all of the tree crops. In February we haven't yet tired of greens and citrus and broccoli and cabbage, but by May we are waiting (not so patiently) for those things to be done and for the peaches and apricots to appear. In our eagerness, we eat them when they are still a bit green.

It can be frustrating for the farmers, having had a long winter's rest, to be patient during this time. They need to get the transplants in the ground, but the risk of frost and ground that is too wet stalls progress, and everyone feels a bit aimless at this time, like we should be doing something, as there are many things to be done, instead of standing still.

And then all of a sudden, the minute the weather turns, the farm bursts into action. It happens so fast we can barely catch our breath before we are hurled into constant activity. The thousands of summer transplants only have a short window to get into the ground. Everything needs watering. Every tractor is in use. The trucks are driving a little faster and everyone moves with purpose. This is the time when we start to buckle down and use that nervous energy we have been saving until this moment. The sun stays up a little later and so do the farmers. This is the time when our year ahead is decided. Much depends on the spring. If it continues to rain too late into April and May, we will be late getting our starts into the ground, and our busiest time will get shortened. Even a week in the spring can make a big difference on where we end up at the end of the year. The earlier we can get to summer, the better our year will be. ***Jenna***

SILKY NANTES CARROT SOUP WITH DILL

SERVES 4 OR 5

1 pound (450 g) carrots (roughly 2 bunches), peeled and sliced into ½-inch (1.3 cm) rounds

2 tablespoons extra-virgin olive oil

1 teaspoon kosher salt

½ teaspoon ground cumin

1 medium onion, diced

4 cloves garlic, roughly chopped

4 cups (950 ml) vegetable stock, chicken stock, or water

2 bay leaves

⅓ cup (6 g) tender dill fronds, stems removed

Extra-virgin olive oil, for garnish

½ teaspoon chile flakes (optional)

Toppings (recipes follow)

We grow exceptional carrots. Our spring carrots are super sweet, thanks to a combination of the Nantes variety, our rich soil, and the cool Capay Valley spring nights. During harvest, some carrots inevitably break or are cosmetically imperfect. These are perfect for transforming into this delightful spring soup. *Jenna*

Preheat the oven to 375°F (190°C).

In a bowl, toss the carrots with 1 tablespoon of the olive oil, the salt, and cumin. Spread them in a single layer on a sheet pan. Roast until lightly browned and tender, about 15 minutes.

Meanwhile, in a heavy-bottomed pot, heat the remaining 1 tablespoon olive oil over medium heat. Add the onion and sauté until translucent and starting to brown, 5 to 7 minutes. Stir in the garlic and cook for an additional minute.

Pour in the stock (or water) and add the bay leaves. Bring to a gentle simmer. Stir in the roasted carrots and cook until the carrots are very soft, 10 to 15 minutes.

Remove the bay leaves and let the soup cool slightly. Blend with an immersion blender or a standard blender until completely smooth. For an extra silky texture, strain the soup through a fine-mesh sieve to remove any fibrous bits. Taste and add more salt, if needed.

Ladle the soup into bowls and garnish with fresh dill, a drizzle of olive oil, and a pinch (or to taste) of chile flakes. Serve immediately, with one of the toppings if you'd like.

TOPPING IDEAS

Fried Chickpeas: Heat 2 tablespoons olive oil in a skillet over medium-high heat. Add one (14-ounce / 400 g) can chickpeas, drained and rinsed. Fry, stirring often, until golden and crisp. Toss with 1 teaspoon ground cumin and ½ teaspoon salt.

Creamy Herbed Yogurt: Mix ½ cup (120 g) Greek yogurt with 1 tablespoon finely chopped mint, 1 tablespoon finely chopped parsley, grated zest of 1 lemon, 2 teaspoons lemon juice, and 1 teaspoon salt.

Torn Croutons: Tear a loaf of bread into bite-size chunks. Toss with olive oil and a pinch of salt. Toast in a hot skillet, stirring often, until golden brown.

Radish and Fennel Crunch: Dice 2 radishes and ¼ fennel bulb. Sprinkle over the soup for a fresh, crisp contrast.

ROASTED BEET, CARROT, AND CITRUS SALAD WITH MINT AND YOGURT

SERVES 4 TO 6

Beets and Carrots

2 tablespoons kosher salt

¼ teaspoon ground cumin

¼ teaspoon freshly ground black pepper

¼ teaspoon chile flakes

4 tablespoons extra-virgin olive oil

10 medium red, gold, or Chioggia beets, washed, trimmed, and cut into wedges

10 to 15 small new carrots, washed and trimmed (7 to 8 if large, peeled and cut into spears)

Citrus

1 navel orange

1 blood orange

1 grapefruit or pomelo

2 small mandarins

Herbs

1 bunch mint, washed

1 bunch Italian parsley, washed

Dressing

1 cup (240 g) yogurt

Grated zest of 1 lemon

Juice of ½ lemon

1 tablespoon extra-virgin olive oil

Assembly

Extra-virgin olive oil

This colorful salad packs a real vitamin C punch and is just what we want to eat when winter gives way to spring. A combination of different beet varieties makes a beautiful salad. I love to leave the skin on the beets. It gives them an earthy flavor when roasted, so take your time scrubbing them clean and trimming any bits that look tough. If you can find beets with the tops on, they are often fresher than storage beets and the skins are much more tender. The herbs are what make it really shine, so don't skimp there. While destemming herbs can be tedious, think of it as meditative and know that it will make a big difference in the end result!

SWAPS/SPINS: **You can omit the yogurt to make it dairy free, opting for some good-quality olive or avocado oil. And for the herbs, we like mint and parsley best, but tarragon is also nice on this salad, or a mix of the three.** *Amon*

Roast the beets and carrots: Preheat the oven to 400°F (200°C).

In a small bowl, combine the salt, cumin, pepper, and chile flakes. Toss the beets with 3 tablespoons (45 ml) of the olive oil and half of the salt mixture and arrange on a sheet pan in a single layer. If using different color beets, try to keep the varieties separate as the colors will run and bleed into each other as they cook.

Roast until fork-tender, 15 to 20 minutes. Remove and let cool slightly.

Toss the carrots with the remaining 1 tablespoon olive oil and all but 1 teaspoon of the remaining salt mixture. Arrange on a sheet pan in a single layer and roast until fork-tender, 10 to 15 minutes. Remove and let cool slightly.

Meanwhile, prepare the citrus: Supreme the orange, blood orange, and pomelo (see How to Supreme Citrus, page 271) into a bowl, squeezing the juice from the membranes into the bowl. For the mandarins, if you are using a variety with a very thin skin, slice paper thin from stem end to blossom end lengthwise with a very sharp knife and place into the bowl with the other citrus, without removing the peel. If the peel is thick, peel before slicing.

Prep the herbs: Pull the leaves off the mint and parsley stems. Finely chop 1 tablespoon or so of each for the dressing. The remainder can be left whole for the salad.

Make the dressing: In a small bowl, combine the yogurt, lemon zest, lemon juice, olive oil, and chopped mint and parsley and stir to combine.

To assemble: Arrange some of the warm beets and carrots on a platter, layer with some of the citrus and herbs. Continue to build the salad until all items have been used. Sprinkle with the reserved salt mixture and drizzle with the dressing.

LAMB CHOPS WITH TANGY CILANTRO AND MINT YOGURT DRESSING

SERVES 4 OR 5

Lamb Chops

¼ cup (40 g) kosher salt

1 teaspoon garlic powder

1 teaspoon freshly ground black pepper

¼ teaspoon ground cumin

8 or 10 lamb loin chops (about 4 ounces / 115 g each)

1 tablespoon extra-virgin olive oil

Yogurt Dressing

1 cup (240 g) yogurt

½ cup (120 ml) olive oil

¼ cup (15 g) chopped fresh parsley

¼ cup (15 g) chopped fresh mint

¼ cup (10 g) chopped fresh cilantro

Grated zest of 1 lemon

Juice of ½ lemon

Fermented Chile Flakes (page 164) or other spicy ground chile pepper (optional), for serving

Serving lamb at a farm dinner can spark meaningful conversations about the origins of our food. While it might be a bit jarring to tour the lambing barn and then sit down to a plate of lamb chops, it's an important connection to make. We've found that this dish often changes the minds of those who think lamb is too gamey. Harvested in spring when lambs are just under a year old, our lamb has a delicate and mild flavor that wins over even skeptical guests. *Jenna & Amon*

Prepare the lamb chops: In a small bowl, combine the salt, garlic powder, black pepper, and cumin. Generously sprinkle this mixture all over the lamb chops. If you have a bit of seasoning left over, don't worry! Save it in a small container for serving alongside the chops. Let the seasoned chops rest for 10 to 15 minutes to absorb the flavors.

Meanwhile, in a large cast-iron or heavy-bottomed skillet, heat the olive oil over medium heat. Once the oil is hot, brown the lamb chops for about 3 minutes on each side, or until a thermometer inserted near the bone reads 130°F (54°C) for medium-rare. Remove the chops from the heat and allow them to rest for 2 to 3 minutes before serving.

While the lamb chops are resting, make the yogurt dressing: In a small bowl, combine the yogurt, olive oil, parsley, mint, cilantro, lemon zest, and lemon juice. Mix well until everything is evenly incorporated. Taste and adjust the seasoning with a pinch of salt if necessary.

To serve, spoon the tangy yogurt dressing over the lamb chops. Sprinkle with fermented chile flakes for a touch of heat, if desired.

LODGE

SPRING EGG PASTA WITH PEA SHOOTS AND CREAM

As an organic farm, we rely on cover crops to replenish our fields, capturing sunlight and converting it into nutrients for future crops. In the winter, we grow vetch, peas, clover, oats, and fava beans to anchor the soil and provide biomass for spring planting. These crops also yield tender pea shoots, which bring a sweet, green flavor to dishes. While pea shoots are lovely in salads, my favorite use is in this simple creamy pasta dish.

SWAPS/SPINS: **To make the dish a bit more substantial, add 1 pound (450 g) of browned Italian sausage, mushrooms, or roasted fennel. If you cannot find pea shoots, we suggest substituting in 1 cup (145 g) shelled English peas and 1 cup (100 g) chopped sugar snap peas.** *Amon*

SERVES 4 OR 5

Kosher salt for the pasta water

1 tablespoon extra-virgin olive oil

1 medium yellow onion, diced

1 small bulb fennel, diced

4 tablespoons (60 g) unsalted butter

2 stalks green garlic, thinly sliced, or 4 cloves garlic, minced

1 cup (240 ml) heavy cream

4 ounces (115 g) soft goat cheese, such as chèvre

2 teaspoons kosher salt

1 teaspoon freshly ground black pepper

Fresh Egg Pasta (page 301), rolled and cut into zigzag pappardelle, or 1 pound (450 g) store-bought pappardelle

2 cups (20 g) packed tender pea shoots

Grated zest and juice of ½ lemon

Finely grated Parmesan cheese

Fill a large soup pot with at least 6 quarts (6 L) salted water and bring to a boil over high heat.

Meanwhile, in a large heavy-bottomed skillet, heat the olive oil over medium heat. Add the onion, fennel, and butter and cook until the onions are translucent, about 6 minutes. Stir occasionally, scraping up any browned bits from the bottom of the pan. Add the garlic and cook for 1 minute more.

Reduce the heat to low and stir in the cream, chevre, salt, and pepper. Simmer the sauce gently, allowing the flavors to meld for 1 minute.

Add the fresh pasta to the boiling water and cook until it floats, 2 to 3 minutes. If using store-bought pasta, follow the cooking directions on the package.

In a large serving bowl or platter, combine the sauce, two-thirds of the pea shoots, and the lemon zest. Drain the pasta and toss it with the sauce and toppings using tongs, ensuring everything is well coated and creamy.

Finish the dish with the lemon juice, some finely grated Parmesan, and the remaining pea shoots. Serve immediately.

PERFECT SAUTÉED GREENS

SERVES 2 OR 3, EASILY DOUBLED TO SERVE 4 TO 6

1 pound (450 g) of your greens of choice (about 1 bunch)

1 tablespoon extra-virgin olive oil

1 clove garlic (optional), sliced paper thin

½ teaspoon kosher salt

½ lemon

The type of greens you are using will dictate their cooking needs. Spinach, arugula, and mizuna are softer and need less time in the pan than do the hardier greens like collards, kale, and chard. I have seen kale recipes that call for cooking the kale for quite a long time over low heat, but personally, I like to cook all the greens minimally, to preserve their color, flavor, and nutritional content. I start with heating oil in a cast-iron skillet. I usually use olive oil, but if I am making a stir-fry, I might add a splash of toasted sesame oil. After adding the greens, I turn the greens frequently with tongs to cook them evenly. I wait until the end to add any toppings, like chèvre or crumbled feta, off the heat. *Jenna*

Tear or cut the greens from the stalk and tear into bite-size pieces. Submerge in water, agitate with your hands, and lift out to drain.

In a cast-iron or nonreactive (stainless or ceramic) sauté pan, heat the oil over high heat. Before the oil gets too hot, add the garlic (if using) and cook for 30 seconds. Add the greens and sauté until wilted. Be careful of hot oil and water, it can be dangerous! Add the salt and squeeze the lemon on top. Serve immediately.

PIZZA WITH LEEK, POTATO, AND ARUGULA

SERVES 2 TO 4

2 balls Pizza Dough (page 297), at room temperature, stretched and ready for toppings

Flour, for dusting

Extra-virgin olive oil, for brushing

1 small leek, trimmed and sliced into rounds ⅛ inch (3 mm) thick

1 stalk green garlic, thinly sliced, or 1 large clove garlic, sliced paper thin

1 medium blue potato, sliced into paper-thin rounds

1 medium German Butterball potato, sliced into paper-thin rounds

2 cups (225 g) ¼-inch (6 mm) cubes mozzarella cheese

1 cup (20 g) torn arugula leaves

4 tablespoons arugula flowers, mustard flowers, or other small edible flowers

Shaved pecorino cheese, for topping

We love the combination of creamy leeks and potatoes with the spicy bite of fresh arugula on this pizza. This pie skips the tomato sauce but is still rich, salty, and delicious. If the arugula doesn't pack enough spice for your taste, a sprinkle of red chile flakes or a splash of hot sauce will do the trick. The toppings listed will be enough for two pizzas. *Amon*

Preheat the oven or grill with a pizza stone to 500°F (260°C). Allow at least 30 minutes for the stone to heat fully. (Or use a pizza oven if you have one.)

Working with one pizza at a time, place the dough on a floured pizza peel or sheet pan. Brush with olive oil, then layer on half of the leek, garlic, and potato slices. Avoid overlapping the potato slices, as thicker layers may not cook through evenly. Top with half of the mozzarella.

Transfer the pizza to the pizza stone (or pizza oven) and bake until the cheese is bubbling and beginning to brown, and the crust is golden, 7 to 10 minutes (or less in a pizza oven). If using your regular oven, carefully lift the corner of the pizza and check to make sure that the bottom is fully cooked.

Remove the pizza from the oven and top with half of the torn arugula leaves, flowers, and shaved pecorino. Slice and serve immediately.

Repeat for the second pizza.

CITRUS TEA CAKE

Some dear friends of ours who own a neighboring farm with a large CSA approached us about creating a seasonal tea cake to offer as an add-on to their boxes. We make this spring tea cake with both oranges and mandarins, depending on what we have available. We blend the entire orange because the peel gives the cake a slightly bitter edge and more depth of flavor. We slather them with a syrup made from orange juice and powdered sugar when they are still hot. This keeps them moist and gives them a nice shine. *Jenna & Amon*

MAKES ONE STANDARD 8½- BY 4½-INCH (20 BY 10 CM) LOAF

Softened butter or oil, for the pan

8 ounces (225 g) whole navel oranges, Valencia oranges, or mandarins

1½ cups (185 g) whole-grain flour (we like Frassinetto)

1 teaspoon baking powder

¾ teaspoon baking soda

¼ teaspoon ground cinnamon

⅛ teaspoon ground cloves

1 cup plus 2 tablespoons (225 g) granulated sugar

1 cup (240 ml) vegetable oil

3 large eggs

¾ teaspoon sea salt

¾ teaspoon vanilla extract

Glaze

½ cup (62 g) powdered sugar

Grated zest of ½ orange

1 tablespoon fresh orange juice, or more as needed

Preheat the oven to 325°F (160°C). Butter or oil the loaf pan.

Roughly chop the oranges and remove any seeds. Add to a blender and pulse until puréed.

Sift the flour, baking powder, baking soda, cinnamon, and cloves together into a bowl. In a stand mixer fitted with the paddle attachment, beat the granulated sugar, oil, and eggs on medium speed for 2 minutes. Add the blended oranges, salt, and vanilla and mix until incorporated.

Fold the dry ingredients into the wet ingredients until no dry flour remains. Pour the mixture into the loaf pan.

Bake until a toothpick inserted in the center comes out clean, 40 to 45 minutes.

While the cake is baking, make the glaze: In a small bowl, whisk together the powdered sugar, orange zest, and orange juice. Add more juice if needed to reach the desired consistency. The glaze should be pourable, and not too thick.

Remove the cake from the oven and while still warm, drizzle and brush with the glaze. Remove the cake from the pan after it has cooled slightly, about 10 minutes. Cool to room temperature before serving.

The cake can be stored in the fridge for up to 10 days in a sealed container. Allow it to come to room temperature before enjoying.

The Farm Kitchen

The Farm Kitchen is our own personal Taj Mahal. It's a testament of love for each other and for a place. We built it from the ground up, on one of the few bare patches of earth at the farm. It wasn't good ground for farming, and the claylike soil cracked in the summer. It was meant to house our growing farm dinner series, events, and a place where the many, many visitors that come to the farm each year could begin their tours or program away from the hustle and bustle of the packing shed, which we lovingly dubbed Grand Central Station. The Kitchen was also the solution to our highly illegal jam and tomato sauce production. We needed a clean, legal space to preserve our first products. We had outgrown the small outdoor kitchen outside of Amon's mom Dru's house.

Our architect and builder, Steve Schroeder, is a local man who also designed the Full Belly Farm office and many other buildings. He hand draws his plans, and his buildings fit into the landscape like they have always been there. In what was either the smartest or dumbest move, we decided to put our house right on top of our kitchen, raising our three kids smack in the middle of the farm. It took us about a year to convince everyone a kitchen was a good idea, two years to design and permit it, and another two years to build it. When we started the building process, I thought my second baby would be born in the house. By the time it was finished I was about to have my third. Sometimes, I still can't believe that we finished this crazy project. Amon hand built several of the larger light fixtures, because by the time we needed them, large light fixtures were no longer in our budget! This building has borne witness to so many happy moments—the birth of my daughter, my second son's first steps, wedding celebrations of all flavors, friends coming together to share a meal and an evening together, children loving on our menagerie of farm dogs, and music. The lawn has been danced on barefoot by thousands of feet, and I feel proud that we created a space that has been home to so much joy for so many people and that we turned that bare patch of ground into an oasis for our immediate and extended community. It is a pleasure to see the same faces year after year at our farm dinners, and watch their families grow up alongside ours. We often have couples who were married here come back to the farm for the farm dinner in the month they were married to celebrate their anniversary. They come back with their babies, who get to drive the tractor with Amon on the farm tour. How amazing that these kids will have a connection to the place where their parents were married.

Of course, it didn't start with us. We wouldn't be here without the very hard work of Dru and Paul, Andrew, and Judith and their own commitment to this farm. They laid the foundation for us, and we continue to build on it, evolving along with the landscape as new babies are born and we turn the corner into middle age and old age. ***Jenna***

RAW ASPARAGUS AND FENNEL SALAD WITH LEMON AND PARMESAN CURLS

SERVES 4

2 pounds (900 g) thick asparagus spears

1 medium bulb fennel

¼ cup (60 ml) good extra-virgin olive oil

Grated zest and juice of 1 lemon

Salt

½ teaspoon freshly ground black pepper

Small chunk of Parmesan cheese

When asparagus first comes into season, it's exciting because its arrival is one of the first signs that spring has definitely sprung and warmer weather is on the way. After a few weeks, my initial enthusiasm starts to wane. It's so easy to just toss some in the oven and roast it, and that's what we do most often. But this version reinvents asparagus, and is good on those first really warm days when you are looking for a cooling salad. *Jenna*

Wash the asparagus by submerging it in water. Using a vegetable peeler, hold an asparagus spear by the root end against the cutting board and peel away from you to create small ribbons, staying away from the root end to avoid the tough woody part of the spear.

Trim the stalks and fronds from the fennel. Halve the fennel bulb lengthwise, lay cut-side down, and slice into very thin strips.

Place the fennel and asparagus into a medium serving bowl. Add the olive oil, lemon zest, lemon juice, salt, and pepper and toss to combine.

Shave curls of Parmesan with the vegetable peeler, you'll want about ½ cup (60 g). Add to the salad and mix again. Top with a bit more Parmesan and then taste and add a bit more salt if needed.

CHOOSING THE BEST ASPARAGUS

When preparing a raw asparagus salad (or any asparagus recipe), selecting and storing the right spears is essential for achieving the best texture and flavor. Here's what to look for:

+ Look for asparagus that is firm, straight, and vibrant in color. The tips should be tightly closed and not wilted or slimy.
+ The spears should "snap" when bent, a sign of peak freshness.
+ For raw salads, thicker stalks are often better. They're tender and require minimal preparation, perfect for shaving into ribbons or slicing thinly.
+ Asparagus is at its best in spring when it's naturally sweeter and more tender. Locally grown asparagus will have superior flavor compared to imported or out-of-season options.
+ Store asparagus upright in a jar with 1 inch (2.5 cm) of water, covered loosely with plastic, and keep it in the fridge. This will maintain freshness for up to 1 week.
+ Avoid washing until ready to use, as moisture can cause spoilage.

Asparagus is an incredible annual plant on our farm that seems to enjoy the hot summers and mild springs. In early March, after our last frost, we will start to see green shoots emerging from the "crown," or underground mass of roots, that has been waiting patiently all winter long to grow. In peak production it can grow up to 6 inches (15 cm) in a day! Freshly harvested asparagus is always the best if you can find it.

ASPARAGUS MINI QUICHES

It's spring, a time of all things adorable. Baby lambs are bouncing around the fields, and a fresh batch of sweet chicks fills the air with their cheerful peeps. These small quiches fit well into spring's "cute" theme. Perfect for appetizers or lunchboxes, these quiches are baked in muffin tins and filled with tender asparagus, Gruyère, and fragrant spring garlic. We partially cook the filling before adding the eggs, ensuring a perfectly balanced bite every time. *Jenna & Amon*

SWAPS/SPINS: **If you'd prefer a full-size quiche, this recipe works just as well in a 9-inch (23 cm) pie tin. Adjust the baking time to 35 to 40 minutes, or until the filling is set and the crust is golden. In this case you will only need one disc of pie dough.**

MAKES 16 MINI QUICHES

Softened butter, for the pan

1 recipe Pie Dough (page 294), chilled as directed

Extra-virgin olive oil

1 small onion (100 g), diced

3 cloves garlic, minced

5 ounces (140 g) thin asparagus, cut into ¼-inch (6 mm) coins (about 1 cup cut), tips reserved for garnish

6 large eggs

1 tablespoon chopped fresh thyme

1 tablespoon chopped fresh parsley

½ teaspoon kosher salt

¼ teaspoon freshly ground black pepper

1 cup (120 g) grated Gruyère cheese

Preheat the oven to 375°F (190°C).

Lightly grease 16 muffin tin wells with butter. Roll out the pie dough on a floured surface to roughly ⅛ inch (3 mm) and cut into 16 rounds slightly larger than the wells of your muffin tins. We like to use the ring from a wide mouth mason jar lid to cut the dough into the correct sized circles. Press the dough into the wells, trimming any excess. Refrigerate for at least 15 minutes to firm up the dough.

In a skillet, warm a drizzle of olive oil over medium heat. Add the onion and garlic and sauté until softened, 3 to 4 minutes.

Add the asparagus coins and cook for 1 minute. Remove from the heat and set aside to cool slightly.

Remove the muffin tins from the refrigerator. Divide the filling evenly among the prepared crusts.

In a bowl, whisk together the eggs, thyme, parsley, salt, and pepper. Pour the egg mixture evenly over the filling and top with the Gruyère.

Top each quiche with a reserved asparagus tip for decoration.

Bake until the filling is set and the crust is golden brown, 20 to 25 minutes.

Allow the mini quiches to cool slightly before removing from the tin. Serve warm or at room temperature.

ROASTED ASPARAGUS WITH POACHED EGGS AND ZA'ATAR BUTTER

SERVES 6

¼ cup (60 ml) distilled white vinegar

4 tablespoons (60 g) salted butter

1 tablespoon za'atar

1 pound (450 g) asparagus, ends snapped

1 tablespoon extra-virgin olive oil

Salt and freshly ground black pepper

6 small eggs, preferably pullet eggs

Crusty bread, for serving

This dish isn't just a side—it's a complete meal. Perfect for a light lunch or brunch, roasted asparagus paired with the richness of poached eggs and the fragrant depth of za'atar butter is as satisfying as it is simple. We use pullet eggs, which are eggs laid by young hens. They are smaller but are quite rich and the right size for this dish. Their firm whites and vibrant yolks make them perfect for poaching; they hold their shape beautifully in simmering water. These eggs poach quickly—just 2 to 2½ minutes for a soft, runny yolk. Freshness is key for a tidy poach, and smaller farm or backyard flocks often provide the best-quality pullet eggs. Look for these gems at farmers' markets or from local ranchers! If you can't find pullet eggs, any fresh eggs will do. *Jenna & Amon*

Set the oven to broil.

Fill a large saucepan at least 9 inches (23 cm) wide with 2 inches (5 cm) water. Add the vinegar and bring to a gentle simmer over medium heat.

In a small saucepan, melt the butter over medium heat. Stir in the za'atar and cook until foamy and just starting to turn golden, 1 to 2 minutes. Remove from the heat and set aside.

In a bowl, toss the asparagus with the olive oil, a pinch of salt, and a few grinds of black pepper. Arrange in a single layer on a sheet pan. Broil until just starting to brown but still firm, 3 to 5 minutes.

While the asparagus is roasting, crack each egg into a separate small bowl or ramekin. Working quickly, gently slide, at water level, one egg at a time into the simmering water. Poach until the whites are set but the yolks are still runny, 2 to 2½ minutes for pullet eggs, or 3 minutes for standard eggs. Remove with a slotted spoon and drain on a clean paper towel.

Arrange the roasted asparagus on a platter or individual plates. Top with the poached eggs and drizzle generously with the za'atar butter.

Serve this dish warm, with a slice of crusty bread to soak up the za'atar butter and runny egg yolk.

FULL BELLY
FARM

ROASTED SPATCHCOCKED CHICKEN WITH LEMON AND ROSEMARY

My grandfather, Art Clemens, wasn't known for his prowess in the kitchen, but it seemed like everyone in Santa Barbara County had tried his lemon chicken at some point. An active member of his church, the local Rotary club, and other community groups, he would make this for a crowd. I remember him spending hours in front of the grill, squirting lemon juice out of a green plastic bottle and sprinkling garlic salt. Amon took the idea and changed it a bit to fit our farm dinner and weddings at the farm. At its heart, though, it is still Grandad's recipe. *Jenna*

SERVES 4 TO 6

1 whole chicken (3 to 4 pounds / 1.3 to 1.8 kg), spatchcocked (see box below)

½ cup (120 ml) fresh lemon juice (about 2 large lemons)

4 cloves garlic, minced

2 sprigs fresh rosemary, plus 1 tablespoon, finely chopped

1 tablespoon kosher salt

1 teaspoon freshly ground black pepper

¼ teaspoon ground cumin

Pinch of chile flakes

2 cipollini onions, cut into quarters

1 lemon, thinly sliced

Place the spatchcocked chicken on a sheet pan and evenly coat with the lemon juice. In a small bowl, combine the garlic, chopped rosemary, salt, pepper, cumin, and chile flakes. Sprinkle the mixture liberally on the chicken, starting on the underside and working your way to the breast side. Arrange the chicken skin-side up and tuck the rosemary sprigs, onion wedges, and lemon slices under and around the chicken. Place the chicken in the fridge, uncovered, for 4 to 12 hours to allow the skin to dry.

Remove the chicken from the fridge at least 30 minutes before roasting, so it can come to room temperature.

Preheat the oven to 425°F (220°C).

Roast the chicken for 20 minutes. Once the chicken just begins to brown, reduce the oven temperature to 225°F (110°C) and continue cooking until the internal temperature reaches 165°F (74°C) in the thickest part of the breast and 175°F (80°C) in the thigh, an additional 40 to 50 minutes. Baste with pan juices halfway through cooking for extra flavor.

Let the chicken rest for 10 minutes before carving. Serve with the roasted lemon slices and pan juices spooned over the top.

SPATCHCOCKING MADE SIMPLE

Removing the backbone of a chicken to flatten it for more even cooking (spatchcocking/butterflying) speeds up roasting time and ensures beautifully crispy skin. To spatchcock:

1. Use sharp kitchen shears to cut along both sides of the backbone and remove it.
2. Flip the chicken over and press firmly on the breastbone to flatten as much as possible.

BLACKENED BROCCOLINI WITH LEMON AND GARLIC CHILE OIL

This fantastic recipe is inspired by Yotam Ottolenghi (one of our very favorite chefs and cookbook authors). Something about the combination of smokiness, zesty lemon juice, and spicy oil works magic here. I promise, if you try it, you won't be disappointed. In the spring we have green garlic, and we love to use that in the chile oil. Your lemons should be cut extremely thin—you should be able to see through them. *Amon*

SWAPS/SPINS: **The original recipe calls for broccoli, and that works just as well. Start with the same weight and trim to bite-size branches. Then blanch in boiling salted water for 1 minute and cold-shock in a bowl of ice water. Drain and dry with paper towels before charring.**

SERVES 6

2 bunches of broccolini (about 2 pounds / 900 g total)

¼ cup (60 ml) olive oil

6 cloves garlic, sliced paper thin

¼ teaspoon chile flakes

2 to 5 dried cayenne or other small red chile peppers, whole, depending on desired spice level

1 lemon, quartered lengthwise and then cut crosswise into very thin, triangular window panes

1 tablespoon fresh lemon juice

1 teaspoon kosher salt

Wash the broccolini and trim off any tough ends of the stems. Pat dry with a kitchen towel.

In a small skillet, heat the olive oil, garlic, chile flakes, and chile peppers over medium heat. Cook until the garlic is just starting to brown. Remove from the heat to prevent further cooking. You want the garlic to be crisp, golden brown, and fragrant.

Preheat a cast-iron skillet, grill, or pizza oven to very hot. Char the broccolini with no oil. It should char on the outside but still be firm on the inside. The idea is to blacken the broccolini as fast as you can without overcooking it. Place in a large bowl.

Add three-quarters of the lemon slices, the olive oil mixture, lemon juice, and salt, and toss.

Serve with the remaining lemon slices on top.

NEW POTATOES WITH SPRING HERBS

SERVES 4

1½ pounds (680 g) new potatoes (the size of golf balls or smaller)

2 tablespoons extra-virgin olive oil

Salt and freshly ground black pepper

1 tablespoon chopped fresh sage

1 tablespoon chopped fresh thyme

1 tablespoon chopped fresh rosemary

2 tablespoons unsalted butter (optional), melted

2 tablespoons chopped fresh Italian flat-leaf parsley, for garnish

One of the first dates that Amon and I had on the farm involved "noodling" potatoes. I don't know where this expression comes from, but that's the word we use for digging new potatoes in the spring before they are ready to be harvested. It essentially refers to stealing the littlest, tenderest potatoes before they have had a chance to size up. As we sell potatoes by the pound, this is frowned upon, but we can't help ourselves as they are a real treat in the spring. These potatoes are the size of golf balls or smaller, and their skins are very delicate. Handle them with care as the skin can easily rub off when you wash them. They don't need much dressing up; they are best with olive oil and/or butter and a large handful of herbs. You can use whatever herbs you have on hand. Sage, mint, thyme, parsley, and oregano (or a mix!) all work well. *Jenna*

Preheat the oven to 375°F (190°C).

Wash the new potatoes carefully, as their skins are delicate. If some are slightly larger than a golf ball, you can halve them to ensure even cooking.

In a large bowl, toss the potatoes with the olive oil, making sure they are evenly coated. Sprinkle with salt and pepper to taste.

Add the sage, thyme, and rosemary to the potatoes and toss again to distribute the herbs evenly.

Spread the potatoes in a single layer on a sheet pan. Roast until the potatoes are golden brown and easily pierced with a fork, 25 to 35 minutes. Shake the pan halfway through to ensure even cooking.

Once the potatoes are roasted, remove them from the oven, drizzle with the melted butter, if using, and sprinkle with fresh parsley. Serve immediately.

POTATO VARIETIES AND THEIR QUALITIES

Here are some of the spring potato varieties we grow on the farm. These varieties have been selected over the years for their flavor, yield, and marketability. Each one has distinct qualities that make it ideal for specific dishes, whether you're roasting, mashing, or making a salad. There are many other varieties out there that have their own unique qualities, these are just some of our favorites.

See photo: Clockwise, starting top left.

BINTJE

A versatile all-purpose potato with a smooth and fluffy texture when baked. Bintje potatoes have a slightly sweet flavor and work well for mashing or creamy potato dishes.

RUSSIAN BLUE

A striking, purple-skinned potato with a firm texture and a slightly nutty, earthy taste. Russian Blues are great for roasting, boiling, or even mashing for a unique twist. Their vivid purple color adds both visual appeal and flavor to any dish.

RUSSIAN BANANA

These small, elongated potatoes have a firm texture and subtly sweet flavor. Their flesh holds up well during roasting or boiling, and they shine in potato salads or side dishes where you want the potato to maintain its shape and texture. We love to make oven fries out of these!

FRENCH FINGERLING

With its rosy-red skin and yellow flesh, this fingerling variety stands out at our market stands. Its texture is perfect for roasting and pan-frying. These potatoes are a favorite side dish to grilled meats.

YELLOW FINN

This waxy potato has a smooth, creamy texture and holds its shape well when cooked. It is ideal for roasting, boiling, or making potato salads. Its delicate flavor is complemented by fresh herbs or buttery dressings.

BELLA ROJA

This early-season potato has a rich, earthy flavor and smooth texture. With their deep red skin, they add a beautiful pop of color to any rustic potato dish.

PORK SAUSAGE AND FENNEL PIZZA

SERVES 2 TO 4

2 balls Pizza Dough (page 297), at room temperature, stretched and ready for topping

Flour, for dusting

6 tablespoons (90 ml) Simple Tomato Sauce (page 155)

1 tablespoon olive oil

½ pound (225 g) fresh pork sausage, casings removed, crumbled into small pieces

½ bulb fennel, thinly sliced

1 small bulb green garlic, thinly sliced, or 2 cloves garlic, minced

2 cups (225 g) cubed (¼ inch / 6 mm) mozzarella or 3 small balls (½ lb / 225 g) fresh mozzarella, torn

½ teaspoon fennel seeds (optional), for extra fennel flavor

¼ teaspoon Fermented Chile Flakes (optional; page 164), for heat

¼ cup (20 g) grated Parmesan cheese, plus more for sprinkling

Fresh parsley or fennel fronds, for garnish

Our love for pizza knows no bounds. With three kids, it makes for such an easy and versatile dinner—and the leftovers can go to school the next day (Bonus!). Plus we can use whatever we've got on hand for toppings. This is one of our favorite combinations, with the rich, savory pork sausage balancing out the sweet fennel.
Amon

Preheat the oven or grill with a pizza stone to 500°F (260°C). Allow at least 30 minutes for the stone to heat fully. (Or use a pizza oven if you have one.)

Working with one pizza at a time, place the dough on a floured pizza peel or sheet pan. Spread half of the tomato sauce and half of the olive oil over the dough. Top with half the crumbled, uncooked pork sausage. Layer on half of the fennel slices, green garlic, and mozzarella. Sprinkle with fennel seeds and chile flakes (if using).

Transfer the pizza to the pizza stone (or the pizza oven) and bake until the sausage is cooked through, the cheese is bubbling and starting to brown, and the crust is golden, 7 to 10 minutes (or less in a pizza oven).

Remove from the oven and sprinkle with half of the freshly grated Parmesan cheese. Garnish with parsley or fennel fronds before slicing and serving. Serve immediately.

Repeat for the second pizza.

CARROT TEA CAKE

This is an everyday cake that goes great with afternoon tea. It's an excuse to eat cake without needing an occasion. No goopy frosting here—just the sweetness of the carrots and nutty, whole-grain flour. The focus is on the sweet spring carrots. You can add walnuts, raisins, or anything else that you like in carrot cake. It's practically a health food. Or at least that's what I tell myself. *Jenna*

MAKES ONE STANDARD 8½- BY 4½-INCH (20 BY 10 CM) LOAF

Butter or oil for the pan

1¼ cups (250 g) sugar

¾ cup (150 g) vegetable oil

2 large eggs

1½ cups (320 g) grated carrots (from about 5 large carrots), grated on the large holes of a box grater

1¼ cups (160 g) whole-grain flour (we like Frassinetto)

1 teaspoon baking soda

1 teaspoon ground cinnamon

½ teaspoon ground nutmeg

½ teaspoon ground ginger

½ teaspoon kosher salt

¼ cup (25 g) chopped walnuts (optional)

Preheat the oven to 325°F (160°C). Grease the loaf pan.

In a large bowl, whisk together the sugar, vegetable oil, and eggs until smooth and creamy. Add the grated carrots and mix well.

In a separate bowl, sift together the flour, baking soda, cinnamon, nutmeg, ginger, and salt. Gradually add the dry ingredients to the carrot mixture, stirring until everything is combined and no dry flour remains.

Pour the batter into the prepared pan, filling it about two-thirds of the way. If using walnuts, sprinkle a small handful on top of the tea cake for extra crunch.

Bake until a toothpick inserted into the center comes out clean, about 40 minutes.

Let the cake cool in the pan for 10 minutes before transferring it to a wire rack to cool completely.

Once cooled, serve the cake as is, or sprinkle with extra walnuts for a nice garnish.

Raising Kids on a Farm

I'll be perfectly honest here. We, like most parents, often feel like we are muddling through. We make the best decisions we can and only in hindsight will we know whether we did right or wrong by our kids (or something in the middle). Here is what I do know. When my youngest was four or five, we went out for a stroll. She was riding her bike, and I was several hundred yards behind her. The chain came off her bike, and I watched her set her bike down on the ground. I figured that was the end of the ride, but then I watched as her small fingers carefully rewound the chain around and she fixed her bike. By the time I got to where she was, she had happily ridden away. That's the thing about farm kids. Their parents are often so busy that they are left to their own devices most of the time, and consequently they have to figure out how to solve a lot of problems on their own and make their own fun. This is not to say they don't sometimes get themselves into lots of mischief as well. We once found them on top of a haystack, sliding down their "hay slide" they had made by cutting the strings of over fifty bales of hay! It took them over a week to clean up.

They also get to experience nature and life cycles in a unique way. For the last four years, we have had a mother owl lay her eggs on our porch. We watch them hatch, and grow, and learn to fly from our living room. They know not to get too attached to the bottle-fed baby lambs, as they don't always make it. They all learned to swim in the swift-moving waters of Cache Creek.

They also sometimes miss out on things that they would have access to if they lived in an urban area. A place to ride a skateboard or rollerblades, lots of play dates with their friends in town, trips to trampoline parks, museums, plays, movie theaters, and other experiences. The pull of those things is real, and sometimes being so far away is hard for them. Certainly, there are trade-offs. Ultimately, I hope that the resilience and self-reliance that they learned growing up on a farm will serve them well when they head out into the world. ***Jenna***

VIBRANT LITTLE GEM SALAD WITH CALENDULA, CHÈVRE, MEMBRILLO, AND LEMON VINAIGRETTE

A few years ago, the Bay Area went crazy for Little Gem lettuce. Sales skyrocketed, and we now make sure to plant plenty for restaurants and markets in the spring. For this salad, we use both red and green varieties. Paired with the floral notes of calendula, creamy chèvre, and the tangy sweetness of membrillo, this salad makes for an eye-catching dish. *Amon*

SERVES 2 TO 4

2 heads Little Gem lettuce, red or green or a combo

1 tablespoon extra-virgin olive oil

1 tablespoon red wine vinegar

1 teaspoon Dijon mustard

Grated zest and juice of 1 lemon

¼ teaspoon sea salt

Freshly cracked black pepper

3½ ounces (100 g) membrillo (quince paste), cut into small cubes (about ½ cup)

3 ounces (85 g) soft goat cheese, such as chèvre, crumbled

¼ cup (3 g) calendula petals (ensure they are food-grade and pesticide-free)

To wash the lettuce, chop the root end off of the head of lettuce, then fill a large bowl with cold water and submerge the leaves. Gently separate all the leaves, discarding any of the outer ones that are torn or bruised. Swish the rest in the water to remove any remaining soil. Lift the lettuce from the bowl and place it in a colander, discarding the water. Repeat the process if necessary. Once clean, use a salad spinner to remove excess water or pat the leaves dry with a clean kitchen towel. This step ensures the lettuce is crisp and free of water, which helps the dressing adhere better. Add the cleaned leaves to a large salad bowl.

In a small bowl, whisk together the olive oil, vinegar, mustard, lemon zest, lemon juice, and sea salt. Season with freshly cracked black pepper to taste. Drizzle the dressing over the lettuce and toss gently to coat the leaves evenly.

Scatter the membrillo cubes, crumbled chèvre, and calendula over the dressed lettuce. Serve immediately.

Note: if your membrillo cubes are sticking together, adding a small amount of olive oil will make them easier to handle.

ROASTED LEG OF LAMB WITH POUNDED GREEN GARLIC AND MINT SALSA VERDE

SERVES 6 TO 8

Lamb

1 bone-in or boneless leg of lamb (4 to 5 pounds / 1.8 to 2.25 kg)

3 tablespoons extra-virgin olive oil

2 tablespoons finely chopped fresh rosemary

1 tablespoon finely chopped fresh thyme

Grated zest of 1 lemon

2 teaspoons kosher salt

1 teaspoon freshly ground black pepper

Salsa Verde

4 medium green garlic stalks, finely minced, including the tender green parts

1 cup (65 g) firmly packed fresh mint leaves, finely chopped

1 cup (65 g) firmly packed fresh parsley leaves, finely chopped

2 tablespoons capers, rinsed and finely chopped

1 anchovy fillet (optional), finely minced

½ cup (120 ml) extra-virgin olive oil

Zest from 1 lemon

2 tablespoons fresh lemon juice

½ teaspoon kosher salt

¼ teaspoon freshly ground black pepper

Amon's mom, Dru, has raised lamb on the farm since the early '90s, and it is a real passion of hers. Our sheep are used both for fiber and meat and are rotated around our fields and on pasture their whole lives, only getting hay when it is too rainy and wet for them to be out and about.

This roasted leg of lamb is a centerpiece-worthy dish, perfect for spring gatherings or holiday meals. The rich, tender meat pairs beautifully with a bright and herbaceous salsa verde made with green garlic and fresh mint. *Jenna*

SWAPS/SPINS: **If you don't have green garlic available, you can also substitute in 6 cloves of garlic.**

Cook the lamb: Preheat the oven to 375°F (190°C).

Pat the leg of lamb dry with paper towels. Rub the lamb all over with the olive oil, then season with the rosemary, thyme, lemon zest, salt, and pepper, ensuring an even coating. Place the lamb on a roasting rack set inside a large baking dish.

Roast the lamb until the internal temperature reaches 130°F to 135°F (54°C to 57°C) for medium-rare or 140°F to 145°F (60°C to 63°C) for medium, 1½ to 2 hours. Baste the lamb occasionally with its juices during cooking to keep it moist.

Once done, remove the lamb from the oven, tent it loosely with foil, and let it rest for 15 to 20 minutes before carving.

Make the salsa verde: In a mortar and pestle (or a bowl with the back of a spoon), combine the green garlic, mint, parsley, capers, and anchovy (if using). Pound or mash until the herbs release their oils and form a rough paste. Stir in the olive oil, lemon zest, lemon juice, salt, and pepper. Adjust seasoning to taste.

Carve the lamb into thin slices and arrange on a serving platter. Spoon the salsa verde over the meat or serve it alongside as a dipping sauce.

STRAWBERRY THYME SHORTCAKES

We often don't have good luck with our strawberries. One year, the deer ate nearly all of the plants in the fall. Another year, we put straw all around the plants, which brought in bugs and made the berries hard to find. This past year, a raccoon started eating the berries long before they turned red! Nonetheless, we continue to plant them because we need something to tide us over between citrus season and stone fruit season. They may not be the biggest money maker for the farm, but they sure do brighten our springtime days, and it is always fun to go out and hunt for ripe strawberries with the kids.

Strawberry shortcake is a springtime classic, and something the kids always ask to make the minute we have a critical mass of strawberries. For this recipe, I use a biscuit instead of a true shortcake. I find that the sweetness of the berries and whipped cream is quite enough, and I prefer a more savory biscuit instead of yet another layer of sweetness. I add thyme to the dough, and no sugar. Strawberries and thyme is a surprising and winning flavor combination. This biscuit also goes well with savory dishes and soups. *Jenna*

MAKES 9 LARGER OR 12 SMALLER SHORTCAKES, DEPENDING ON HOW YOU CUT YOUR BISCUITS

Biscuits

3 tablespoons (30 g) cornmeal

2 cups (240 g) all-purpose flour

2 tablespoons fresh thyme leaves, finely chopped

1½ teaspoons kosher salt

½ teaspoon baking soda

½ cup (115 g) unsalted butter, cut into small chunks and chilled (freeze for best results)

1 cup (240 ml) milk or buttermilk

Strawberries

4 cups (665 g) sliced (¼ inch/6 mm thick) hulled strawberries

½ cup (100 g) sugar

Squeeze of fresh lemon juice

Whipped Cream

1 cup (240 ml) cold heavy whipping cream

2 tablespoons powdered or granulated sugar

½ teaspoon vanilla extract

Make the biscuits: Preheat the oven to 450°F (230°C). Line a sheet pan with parchment paper or butter it lightly. Sprinkle 2 tablespoons of the cornmeal over the sheet.

In a food processor or medium bowl, combine the flour, thyme, salt, and baking soda. Add the butter chunks and pulse in the food processor, or cut them in with a pastry cutter or fork, until the mixture resembles coarse crumbs.

Add the milk and gently fold with a spatula until just combined. Avoid overmixing.

continued

Strawberry Thyme Shortcakes, continued

Turn the dough out onto a floured surface and shape it into a square about 1 inch (2.5 cm) thick. Using a knife or bench scraper, cut the dough in half and stack one half on top of the other. Press gently into another square and repeat this process three to four times to create flaky layers that will easily pull apart when baked.

Transfer the dough to the prepared sheet pan. Sprinkle the remaining 1 tablespoon cornmeal over the top and cut into roughly 2-inch (5 cm) squares.

Bake until golden brown, about 15 minutes.

Set the pan on a cooling rack and let cool completely before assembling.

Macerate the strawberries: In a bowl, toss together the strawberries, sugar, and lemon juice. Stir to dissolve the sugar, then refrigerate to macerate until ready to use.

Make the whipped cream: In a stand mixer fitted with the whisk, whip the heavy cream on medium-high speed until soft peaks form. Add the sugar and vanilla and whip to your desired consistency (we like the softest of peaks). Keep refrigerated until serving.

Once the biscuits have cooled, gently pull them apart at the center (the layers should make this easy). Place a layer of macerated strawberries on the bottom half of each biscuit. Add a generous dollop of whipped cream, then top with the other biscuit half. Serve immediately and enjoy!

STRAWBERRY CITRUS PAVLOVA

MAKES 8 TO 10 MINI PAVLOVAS OR ONE 9-INCH (23 CM) PAVLOVA

Meringue

4 large egg whites

1 cup (200 g) granulated sugar

1 teaspoon vanilla extract

1 teaspoon fresh lemon juice

1 teaspoon cornstarch

Topping

1 pint (about 400 g) strawberries, hulled and sliced

3 mandarins, peeled and cut into pieces

2 tablespoons sugar

1 to 2 sprigs fresh lemon verbena, leaves picked and finely chopped

1 cup (240 ml) freshly whipped cream, lightly sweetened or unsweetened

This dessert has endless potential—you can use any combination of fruit on top. The meringues can be made ahead of time, kept in an airtight container for several days. Once you top them with fruit, they will absorb the juices, so that step should happen right before you serve. My daughter Hazel always asks for this on her birthday with the meringues stacked up in place of cake layers. *Jenna*

Make the meringue: Preheat the oven to 250°F (120°C). Line a sheet pan with parchment paper and draw a 9-inch (23 cm) circle on the paper if making a large meringue or several smaller circles for individual servings. For smaller meringues, I use the lid of a wide mouth mason jar to make my circles, which is approximately 3 inches (7.5 cm) wide. You can also free form this. Once you have drawn circles, flip the paper over so the circles are underneath.

In a stand mixer fitted with the whisk (or in a large bowl with a hand mixer), beat the egg whites at medium speed until soft peaks form. Gradually add the sugar, a tablespoon at a time, and continue beating until stiff, glossy peaks form. This may take 5 to 7 minutes. Add in the vanilla and lemon juice and sift the cornstarch over the top, then gently fold together. This helps stabilize the meringue and adds a slight tanginess to complement the sweetness of the fruit.

Spoon the meringue mixture onto the prepared sheet pan, shaping it into a round (for the large pavlova) or individual nests inside the circle(s). Smooth the sides and top, making a small well in the center, which will eventually hold the fruit.

Bake the meringue(s) until crisp on the outside but soft and marshmallow-like inside, 1 hour for smaller meringues or 1½ to 2 hours for a large pavlova. Turn off the oven and let the meringue(s) cool completely in the oven with the door slightly ajar.

Make the topping: Place the sliced strawberries and mandarin pieces in a bowl. Sprinkle with the sugar and lemon verbena. Let the fruit macerate for 15 to 20 minutes to release its juices and intensify the flavors.

Once the meringue has cooled, spoon the macerated fruit mixture on top. Dollop with whipped cream.

Serve immediately.

FRESH MINT CHIP ICE CREAM

At our monthly pizza nights at the farm, I'll make two or three different kinds of ice cream to sell. I always ask my kids what they think I should make and without fail they ask for this one, even if I already made it in the previous month. Using fresh mint and not an extract makes such a difference. My favorite is a Persian mint with very delicate, soft leaves and stems. It only grows in one place on the farm, which is our co-owner's garden, so in the spring I am often caught snooping around in search of enough Persian mint for this ice cream. If you use a stronger, spearmint type mint, the steeping time might be less. Taste as you go along.

We use David Lebovitz's foolproof method for making the custard. In his ice cream bible, *The Perfect Scoop*, he discusses in detail the science behind ice cream, which was so helpful when we began our pizza night ice cream endeavors. *Jenna*

SWAPS/SPINS: **You can also substitute lightly crushed peach leaves for the mint for an almond-y ice cream! If you decide to give peach leaves a go, the steeping time is much less (start with 10 minutes before you start tasting).**

MAKES ABOUT 1 QUART (1 L)

2 cups (480 ml) heavy whipping cream

1 cup (240 ml) whole milk

¾ cup (150 g) sugar

Pinch of kosher salt

2 cups (70 g) tightly packed fresh mint leaves (Persian mint recommended, but spearmint works too)

5 large egg yolks

½ cup (90 g) finely chopped dark chocolate (preferred) or roughly chopped bittersweet chocolate chips

In a medium saucepan, combine 1 cup (240 ml) of the cream, the milk, sugar, and a pinch of salt. Pour the remaining 1 cup (240 ml) cream into a bowl and place in the fridge to stay cold.

Heat the milk and sugar mixture over medium heat, stirring occasionally, until the mixture is steaming but not boiling. Remove from the heat and add the mint leaves. Steep for 45 to 60 minutes, depending on how strong you want the mint flavor. Taste as you go and adjust steeping time to your preference.

Meanwhile, in a separate bowl, whisk the egg yolks until light and smooth.

continued

Fresh Mint Chip Ice Cream, continued

When the mint is finished steeping, remove the leaves with a sieve or spoon, and reheat the mixture. Slowly add a ladle of hot milk mixture to the yolks, a little at a time, while whisking constantly to temper the eggs. Repeat this twice. After you have added three ladles full of the hot milk mixture to the egg yolks, add the warmed yolks to the saucepan with the rest of the milk. Cook over medium-low heat, stirring constantly with a wooden spoon or heatproof spatula. Continue cooking until the mixture thickens and coats the back of the spoon (or until it reaches 180°F / 82°C), 5 to 7 minutes. Be sure not to let it boil.

Once thickened, set a fine-mesh sieve over the bowl with the remaining cup of cold cream, and strain the custard through the sieve into the bowl. Refrigerate for at least 2 hours, or overnight, until well chilled.

Once the custard is chilled, pour it into an ice cream maker and churn according to the manufacturer's instructions. This usually takes 20 to 25 minutes, depending on the machine.

When the ice cream is nearly done, fold in the chopped chocolate (see Note).

Transfer the ice cream to an airtight container and freeze for at least 4 hours, or until firm.

NOTE:

If you prefer, you can also drizzle melted chocolate into the ice cream during the last few minutes of churning for a ribbon effect.

PEACH LEAF CRÈME BRÛLÉE

SERVES 6

2 cups (480 ml) heavy cream

10 fresh peach leaves, rinsed

1 vanilla bean, split, or 1 teaspoon vanilla extract

6 large egg yolks

⅓ cup (67 g) granulated sugar, plus 6 tablespoons for brûléeing

Pinch of kosher salt

This recipe came to us via one of our many Chez Panisse cookbooks. Peaches and almonds are related, and crumpled up peach leaves have a delicious, almond-y scent. This is a wonderful dessert for those months when citrus has finished (or you are tired of it) but the stone fruit isn't in yet. We often serve it at farm dinners in the spring when the weather is warm. The first time we tried it, circa 2011, we had a small backyard dinner and had about thirty servings to brûlée. We had a small kitchen torch that was just not up to the job. About ten servings in, the torch gave up and we were in a panic. Luckily, the farm's mechanic shop was around the corner, and we grabbed an industrial cutting torch. While we wouldn't suggest using a cutting torch to do your brûléeing, we can confidently say it will work in a pinch!

We love this flavor so much we have started infusing other desserts with peach leaves. Peach leaf panna cotta and ice cream are other peach leaf desserts to try. *Jenna*

In a medium saucepan, combine the heavy cream and peach leaves. Scrape in the vanilla seeds and add the vanilla pod (if using vanilla extract, add it later). Heat the mixture over medium heat until it begins to steam and simmer but is not yet boiling. Remove from the heat, cover, and let the leaves steep for 10 minutes to infuse their flavor. Taste it at this point. You can leave it a bit longer, but too long and it will taste bitter. There is a fine line between perfect and bitter, so taste often as you go.

Preheat the oven to 325°F (160°C).

Strain out the peach leaves and vanilla pod from the cream. In a medium bowl, whisk together the egg yolks, ⅓ cup (67 g) sugar, and the salt until the mixture is pale and thickened. Gradually whisk the warm infused cream into the egg mixture, a little at a time, to temper the eggs. Strain the custard through a fine-mesh sieve into a clean bowl or pitcher to ensure a smooth texture. If you're using vanilla extract, add it now.

Divide the custard evenly among six 6-ounce (190 ml) ramekins. Place the ramekins in a large roasting pan or baking dish. Pour hot water into the pan to come halfway up the sides of the ramekins to create a water bath. Cover the entire pan with aluminum foil. Carefully transfer the pan to the oven.

Bake until the custards are set but still slightly jiggly in the center, 30 to 35 minutes. Be careful moving the pan because you do not want the water to get into the custard.

Remove the ramekins from the water bath and allow them to cool to room temperature. Cover and refrigerate for at least 4 hours or overnight.

Just before serving, sprinkle 1 tablespoon of sugar evenly over the top of each custard. Use a kitchen torch to caramelize the sugar until it is golden brown and crisp. (Alternatively, place the ramekins under a broiler for 1 to 2 minutes, watching carefully to prevent burning.)

Let the caramelized tops cool for a minute to harden, then serve immediately.

NAVEL ORANGE MARMALADE

Marmalade is labor-intensive, but it sure is nice to have throughout the year. This is a classic marmalade made with navel oranges and tart lemons, creating a perfectly balanced spread. You can choose if you prefer a thin-cut or thick-cut marmalade and adjust how wide your orange peel strips are to suit your taste. We like a medium cut of about ¼ inch (6 mm), but I have seen lovely versions with very thin strips and more robust versions with thicker than that. Have fun! *Amon*

MAKES ABOUT NINE (8-OUNCE / 250 ML) JARS

2 pounds (900 g) navel oranges

2 pounds (900 g) lemons (Lisbon or Eureka)

3½ pounds (1.6 kg) or a scant 8 cups granulated sugar

Trim the ends off the oranges down to the flesh. Cut in half lengthwise. Take the halves and lay them cut-side down and cut again lengthwise. Slice them into thin ¼-inch (6 mm) segments so you end up with ¼ rounds. Remove any seeds. Place the segments in a large nonreactive pot and cover with water until they just start to float. Let the oranges soak for 4 to 5 hours or overnight.

Cut the lemons into eighths and place them in a separate large nonreactive pot. Remove any seeds. Cover with water until they just start to float. Let the lemons soak for 4 to 5 hours or overnight.

After soaking the oranges, bring them to a boil with their liquid and simmer for 20 minutes. Cover the pot and leave the mixture at room temperature for 4 to 5 hours or overnight.

After soaking the lemons, bring them to a boil with their liquid and simmer until the mixture is slightly syrupy, 1½ to 2 hours. Pour the mixture into a sieve set over a bowl. Cover the sieve and let drain for 4 to 5 hours or overnight.

continued

Navel Orange Marmalade, continued

The next day, in a wide heavy-bottomed pot, combine the strained lemon liquid, cooked oranges and their liquid, and sugar. Stir until the sugar is dissolved. Bring the mixture to a boil over medium-high heat, then reduce to a simmer. Cook, stirring occasionally, until the marmalade reaches a temperature of 220°F (105°C) or passes The Wrinkle Test (below), usually 30 to 40 minutes. Skim off any foam that forms on the surface.

Carefully ladle the hot marmalade into sterilized canning jars, leaving ¼ inch (6 mm) of headspace. Wipe the rims clean, seal with lids and bands, tightening to fingertip tightness. Process in accordance with the jar manufacturer's instructions.

Allow the jars to cool to room temperature. Store in a cool, dark place for up to 1 year. Once opened, refrigerate and use within a few weeks.

TESTING JAM

The Wrinkle Test

1. Place 2 to 3 small plates in the freezer just before you start cooking your jam.
2. When you are ready to test the jam, drop a spoonful of hot jam onto a cold plate and let it sit for 30 seconds.
3. Make a line through the middle of the jam with your finger or a spoon, if the jam wrinkles and holds its shape and does not come back together, the jam is ready.
4. If the jam comes back together and does not wrinkle, continue to cook for a few more minutes and retest on a new cold plate.

DEHYDRATED ORANGES AND MANDARINS

Preserve the amazing flavors of citrus with these dehydrated orange and mandarin slices. They're perfect for garnishing cocktails, enhancing teas, or enjoying as a snack. The mandarins are a great salad topper! This recipe provides two methods tailored to each fruit to bring out their best qualities. *Amon*

MAKES ½ POUND (225 G)

Dehydrated Oranges

2 pounds (900 g) navel oranges

Dehydrated Mandarins

2 pounds (900 g) mandarins

1 tablespoon (14 g) citric acid

For oranges: Wash the oranges thoroughly under cold running water and slice into rounds ⅛ to ¼ inch (3 to 6 mm) thick using a sharp knife or mandoline. Discard any seeds.

For mandarins: Wash the mandarins thoroughly under cold running water, peel, and separate into segments. In a large bowl, dissolve 1 tablespoon of citric acid in 1 quart (950 ml) water. Submerge the segments for 4 to 5 minutes and then remove with a slotted spoon.

DEHYDRATOR METHOD:

Place the slices/segments in a single layer on dehydrator trays, ensuring they don't overlap.

Set a dehydrator to 135°F (57°C). Dry, checking periodically, until the slices/segments are dry but slightly pliable, 8 to 12 hours for oranges, 10 to 14 hours for mandarins.

OVEN METHOD:

Arrange the slices/segments on wire racks set over sheet pans.

Preheat the oven to its lowest setting (around 150°F / 65°C), with convection if possible. If your lowest oven temperature is higher than 150°F, set it to the lowest setting and crack it open with a spoon. Bake the slices/segments until dry but slightly pliable, 6 to 8 hours for oranges, 8 to 10 hours for mandarins, flipping halfway through for even drying.

Let the slices/segments cool completely at room temperature to prevent condensation. Store in an airtight container in a cool, dark place for up to 6 months.

SIMPLE STRAWBERRY JAM

MAKES EIGHT TO NINE (8-OUNCE / 250 ML) JARS

4 pounds (1.8 kg) strawberries

6 cups (1.2 kg) granulated sugar

¾ cup (180 ml) fresh lemon juice

This jam captures the essence of peak-season berries, balanced with a touch of lemon to enhance their natural sweetness. Perfect for spreading on toast, swirling into yogurt, or as a filling for baked goods, this jam is a pantry essential. *Amon*

Hull and rinse the strawberries, then place them in a large, wide, heavy-bottomed pot. Add the sugar and 7 tablespoons (105 ml) of the lemon juice to the pot.

Heat the mixture slowly over medium heat, stirring occasionally, until the strawberries release their juices and the sugar dissolves completely.

Increase the heat to bring the mixture to a rolling boil. Boil hard for 20 to 30 minutes, stirring frequently to prevent sticking or scorching. The strawberries should soften and become saturated with the syrup.

Add the remaining 5 tablespoons (75 ml) lemon juice to the pot. Continue boiling for an additional 5 minutes, stirring constantly.

To check if the jam is set, see Testing Jam on page 72. When your jam is ready, remove the pot from the heat and let it rest for a minute without stirring. Skim off any foam from the surface using a spoon.

Carefully ladle the hot jam into sterilized canning jars, leaving ¼ inch (6 mm) of headspace. Wipe the rims clean, seal with lids and bands, tightening to fingertip tightness. Process in accordance with the jar manufacturer's instructions.

Allow the jars to cool to room temperature. Store in a cool, dark place for up to 1 year. Once opened, refrigerate and use within a few weeks.

MULBERRY JAM

We only have six Pakistani mulberry trees at the farm, but when they ripen, the trees are dripping with fruit all at once. They are extremely popular at the farmers' markets, but even so, we often can't keep up and end up turning some of them into jam. This simple mulberry jam highlights the sweet, tart, and slightly earthy flavor of fresh mulberries. If you have access to excess mulberries, try this recipe out to hang onto their flavor past their very brief season. ***Amon***

MAKES FOUR OR FIVE (8-OUNCE / 250 ML) JARS

2 pounds (900 g) fresh mulberries, rinsed and stems removed (see Note)

4 cups (800 g) granulated sugar

5 tablespoons (75 ml) fresh lemon juice (about 2 small lemons)

Place the cleaned mulberries in a large heavy-bottomed saucepan. Add the sugar and lemon juice and stir to combine.

Slowly heat the mixture over medium heat, stirring frequently until the sugar dissolves and the mixture begins to simmer.

Increase the heat to medium-high and bring the jam to a boil. Continue boiling for 20 to 30 minutes, stirring constantly to prevent sticking.

The jam is ready when it reaches 220°F (105°C) on a thermometer or it passes The Wrinkle Test (see Testing Jam, page 72).

Remove the jam from the heat and skim off any foam. Carefully ladle the hot jam into sterilized canning jars, leaving ¼ inch (6 mm) of headspace at the top. Wipe the rims clean, seal with lids and bands, tightening to fingertip tightness. Process in accordance with the jar manufacturer's instructions.

Allow the jars to cool to room temperature. Store in a cool, dark place for up to 1 year. Once opened, refrigerate and use within a few weeks.

Note: A tomato mill can greatly speed up this process.

A Goat Ate the Tax Return and Other Adventures in Animal Husbandry

Dru, Amon's mother, used to milk goats for her family's milk consumption. One year, many years ago, she received a tax refund and put it in her back pocket and went out to do the morning milking. While she was focused on her task, the goat was focused on the tantalizing piece of paper in her back pocket, and before she knew it her tax refund was half eaten. Imagine trying to explain that to the IRS!

Our animals make up an important part of our landscape here at the farm. Our roughly 2,000 chickens and 300 sheep move about from field to field, building our soils and giving us wool, protein, and occasional comedic relief. The school groups that come to our farm always enjoy getting to know our animals. They get to bottle-feed our "bummer" lambs (those that need to be hand fed for one reason or another) and collect eggs from the chickens. One year we had a school group visiting and Dru was doing a cow milking demonstration. One of the students asked her what kind of milk it was. She replied that it was cow's milk. "Right," said the student, "But I mean what *kind* of milk. Is it like 2% or chocolate milk or skim?" All I can say is, sign me up for the chocolate milk cow, please!

Our animals live really happy lives here (although the sheep start to look a bit grumpy in August when it is hot). They have space to roam and good food to eat. The chickens and the sheep both have their own guard dogs to keep them safe from the many predators that live in our area. Having animals requires a 7-day-a-week, 365-day-a-year commitment to their care. When visitors to the farm see the baby lambs in the spring, they often offer to take one home and I always say, "Be my guest!! You can take one of the bottle-fed ones!" So far, nobody has actually taken me up on this. Animals have needs on Sundays, on Christmas, on Thanksgiving, and every other day of the year. Being in the livestock business is challenging and time-consuming, sometimes joyful and sometimes heartbreaking. In the end, we feel like including animals in our farm plan contributes so much to our biodiversity that we will continue doing lamb checks at 3:00 a.m. and bottle-feeding a few babies every year. ***Jenna***

SUMMER

EARLY SUMMER

MIDSUMMER

LATE SUMMER

PRESERVING SUMMER

SUMMER

No matter how many summers you live here, the first 100°F day hits hard. At some point in the summer, 100°F won't phase us much. When it is 112°F (44°C) for a week straight, "only" 100°F will seem positively pleasant. But that first day isn't easy and always feels like a surprise, even when you know it's coming. Breathing feels hard. The ground dries out so quickly, and cracks form in the earth. In the summer, we start talking a lot about water. What needs water, where we are using too much water, how to conserve water, and the quality of the water. Managing water in the summer is a constant battle. It is a marathon to keep everything alive during the long summer months.

The daylight stretches out and so do our working hours. You can often find us sweaty, tired, and dusty at the end of the day. Sometimes our supper consists of a half of a watermelon, squirreled away in a cooler early in the day. We often do not cook much in the summer. You will notice that we have very little meat in this section. There are two reasons for this: First, we are often just too exhausted to think about preparing a meal, and second, there is such abundance on the farm in the summer and much of what we have available is best eaten raw or minimally cooked. Buttery corn on the cob, peaches that drip juice down your chin, flavorful tomatoes and myriad melons of all colors and textures. The easy-to-prepare food of summer is something we look forward to every year.

The abundance is the trade-off for the heat that we endure in the summer months. All the work that we have poured into the farm in the spring finally pays off, and we have more produce than we know what to do with. Most farms make most of their income during these long, hot days. Ours is no exception. We know that this is the time to hustle. This is the time to buckle down and push through the long days, when the sweat runs down our backs and the dust clings to our skin. This summer abundance will allow us to keep our crew on staff year-round, and we push as hard as we can to pick and pack out thousands of boxes each day. We know it won't last forever, although it sometimes feels that way. This is not to say that summer isn't also full of fun. It is the time for lazy afternoon floats down the creek, after-work tomato fights, Monday-night volleyball games with neighbors, smashing melons open in the middle of a field and scooping out the flesh with bare hands, and ice cream from the Corner Store in Guinda. ***Jenna***

LEMON VERBENA ICED TEA

SERVES 8 TO 10

2 ounces (60 g) fresh lemon verbena leaves (about 2 large handfuls)

½ cup (100 g) sugar or honey, or to taste

Ice

Lemon verbena sprigs or lemon slices, for garnish

This simple recipe is refreshing and hydrating on hot days. We usually make a big batch for a farm dinner and sip on it the following week. Lemon verbena is a really interesting and unique flavor. It is citrus-y without being sour. You can also make a hot tea with this herb, but we like it best on the hottest days, over ice. We have very few verbena plants on the farm, maybe ten or so total, but they grow quickly and like to be cut back frequently, so we never run out. You can also make this with dried verbena leaves if you can't find any fresh leaves. Lemon verbena also has therapeutic benefits, and is often used to ease digestion, reduce stress, and promote restful sleep. *Amon*

In a large pot, bring 1 gallon (3.75 L) water to a boil. Remove from the heat and add the lemon verbena leaves. Cover and steep for 15 to 20 minutes, depending on desired strength.

While the tea is still warm, stir in the sugar or honey until completely dissolved. Adjust the sweetness to your preference.

Strain the tea into a pitcher (discard the lemon verbena leaves). Let it cool to room temperature, then refrigerate until chilled.

Fill glasses with ice and pour the tea over. Garnish with a sprig of fresh lemon verbena or a slice of lemon for an extra touch of summer charm.

CRISP GREEN BEANS WITH GARLIC AND SESAME

Every year at our crop planning meeting, we talk about cutting green beans out of the mix of things that we grow. Hand picking them is very labor intensive. This inefficiency means that they are not suitable for our wholesale market, and so you can only find them at our farmers' market and in our CSA boxes. Though we always threaten to stop growing them, so far, we have not taken that step because they are spectacularly good in early summer.
Amon

SERVES 4

Kosher salt

1 pound 5 ounces (600 g) fresh small tender green beans, trimmed top and bottom

3 tablespoons (45 ml) extra-virgin olive oil

1 tablespoon toasted sesame oil

3 cloves garlic, thinly sliced (use a mandoline for even slices)

2 tablespoons sesame seeds, toasted

½ lemon

Set up a large bowl of ice and water and place it near the stove. Bring a pot of salted water to a boil. Add the green beans and cook until they are tender-crisp, about 2 minutes. Drain and immediately transfer the beans to the ice water to stop the cooking process. Drain again and pat dry.

In a large skillet, heat the olive oil and sesame oil over medium-high heat. Add the thinly sliced garlic and sauté until golden and fragrant, 1 to 2 minutes. Be careful not to burn the garlic.

Add the green beans to the skillet with the garlic and toss to coat in the oils. Cook, stirring occasionally, for 1 to 2 minutes.

Sprinkle the sesame seeds over the green beans and toss to combine. Squeeze the lemon half over the dish and season with salt to taste. Serve immediately.

BLISTERED JIMMY NARDELLO PEPPERS

SERVES 4 AS AN APPETIZER OR SIDE

1 pound (450 g) Jimmy Nardello peppers, shishito, padrone, or other sweet frying peppers peppers

2 tablespoons extra-virgin olive oil

Coarse sea salt

Jimmy Nardello peppers are a celebration of simplicity and heritage, offering a burst of summer sweetness in every bite. Brought to the US by Italian immigrants in 1887, the seeds for these peppers were eventually donated to the Seed Savers Exchange in the late twentieth century. When people are first introduced to them, the first thing they usually ask is: "Are they hot?!" While they look like they might pack a punch, they are not at all spicy. These sweet, slender peppers have become a favorite at our farmers' markets and by local chefs for their versatility and incredible flavor. Their thin skin and tender flesh make them ideal for quick, high-heat cooking methods like grilling or roasting. When cooked, their natural sweetness intensifies, and they develop a smoky, caramelized flavor that's amazing. This simple recipe highlights their best qualities, letting the peppers shine with just a few complementary ingredients.

You can also use this recipe for other peppers, such as shishito. They are perfect for snacking or as a side to grilled meats or fish. The simplicity of olive oil and salt allows the sweet, slightly smoky flavor of the peppers to come through with every bite. Enjoy!
Amon

SERVE WITH: **Crusty bread or alongside grilled meats and cheeses for a complete meal.**

Rinse the peppers and pat them dry. Leave them whole, including the stems, as it adds a handle to eat them with and they look stunning on the plate.

Heat a grill or large skillet over medium-high heat. If sautéeing, add the olive oil and swirl to coat the bottom of the pan. Add the peppers to the hot skillet in a single layer. Sauté, tossing occasionally, until the peppers are blistered and slightly charred on all sides, 4 to 5 minutes. For the grill, toss the peppers in the oil and salt in a small bowl and then place the peppers directly on the grill grates and cook, turning occasionally, until they are blistered and slightly charred all over.

Once the peppers are cooked, sprinkle with salt to taste. Serve immediately while they're warm.

CLASSIC MARGHERITA PIZZA

A timeless favorite, the Margherita pizza is a celebration of simple, fresh ingredients. The combination of tomato sauce, creamy mozzarella, and fragrant basil never gets old. This pizza is proof that sometimes, less is more. *Amon*

SERVES 2 TO 4

2 balls Pizza Dough (page 297), at room temperature, stretched and ready for topping

Flour, for dusting

Extra-virgin olive oil, for brushing

½ cup (120 ml) Simple Tomato Sauce (page 155)

10 to 15 fresh basil leaves, torn or left whole

8 ounces (225 g) fresh mozzarella, cut into ¼-inch (6 mm) cubes or torn into bite-size pieces

Pinch of sea salt or red chile flakes (optional)

Preheat the oven or grill with a pizza stone to 500°F (260°C). Allow at least 30 minutes for the stone to heat fully. (Or use a pizza oven if you have one.)

Working with one pizza at a time, place the dough on a floured pizza peel or sheet pan. Brush the dough lightly with olive oil. Spread half the tomato sauce evenly over the surface, leaving a ½-inch (1.3 cm) border around the edges. The classic debate about when to add the basil happens now. I personally like to add the leaves now and then scatter half the mozzarella cubes or torn pieces evenly over the top. Or some folks like to wait until after the pizza is cooked to add the torn basil. Either way is good!

Transfer the pizza to the pizza stone (or pizza oven) and bake until the cheese is bubbling and beginning to brown, and the crust is golden and crisp, 5 to 7 minutes (or less in a pizza oven).

Remove the pizza from the oven and immediately top with fresh basil leaves (if you haven't already). Drizzle lightly with olive oil. If desired, sprinkle with a pinch of sea salt or red chile flakes. Slice and serve the pizza immediately.

Repeat for the second pizza.

ZUCCHINI AND SWEET CORN CAKES

SERVES 4

1 cup (150 g) grated zucchini

1 cup (150 g) sweet corn kernels, fresh or frozen

2 cloves garlic, minced

1½ cups (210 g) Bloody Butcher cornmeal (or any coarse cornmeal)

1 cup (120 g) all-purpose flour

2 large eggs

½ to 1 large jalapeño, deseeded and finely chopped

2 tablespoons chopped fresh chives

Salt and freshly ground black pepper

6 tablespoons (85 g) unsalted butter, melted

Pepper Sauce

½ cup (120 g) sour cream

½ cup (120 g) full-fat yogurt

1 mild red chile, minced

1 mild green chile, minced

Juice of 1 lime

Pinch of kosher salt and freshly ground pepper

This dish is a substantial and filling appetizer. We use our red Bloody Butcher cornmeal in combination with a regular flour to bump up the flavor profile. This is also a great way to use some of the zucchini abundance that home gardeners and farmers alike face each year. We like to amp up the spice with a creamy, colorful pepper sauce. *Amon*

In a large bowl, combine the zucchini, corn, garlic, cornmeal, flour, eggs, jalapeño, and chives. Stir until everything is well incorporated. Season with salt and black pepper.

Heat a nonstick skillet over medium heat and add 1 to 2 tablespoons of melted butter. Once the butter is hot, spoon 2 to 3 tablespoons of the fritter batter into the skillet, gently flattening each mound with the back of the spoon. Cook until golden brown and crispy on both sides, 3 to 4 minutes per side. Remove the cooked fritters to a warm plate. Repeat with the remaining batter, adding more butter as needed.

Make the pepper sauce: In a small bowl, stir together the sour cream, yogurt, chiles, lime juice, salt, and pepper.

Place a small dollop of the sauce on top of each cake and enjoy!

FIG LEAF ICE CREAM

MAKES 1 QUART (1L)

3 fresh fig leaves (young and tender), washed, dried, de-stemmed, toasted, and roughly chopped (about ⅓ cup or 8 g)

¾ cup (150 g) granulated sugar

7 egg yolks

1 cup (240 ml) whole milk

2 cups (480 ml) heavy cream

Pinch of kosher salt

There's a brief window in spring and early summer when fig leaves are tender, vibrant green, and fragrant—before the summer sun turns them leathery and tough. We started making fig leaf ice cream years ago, drawn to its subtle tropical notes—think green coconut and warm vanilla.

A chef visiting from Chez Panisse suggested we try toasting the leaves before steeping them in the cream. A few seconds over an open flame, and the aroma deepened—suddenly there was toasted coconut, caramel, something almost nutty in the air. It added a new dimension and some warmth. The toasting does not take long. A few passes over a flame will do it. *Amon & Jenna*

Toast the fig leaves briefly (2 to 3 seconds on each side) over an open flame or in a dry skillet. They should be toasted until fragrant and slightly blistered. Let cool, then remove any large ribs and roughly chop. In a food processor, pulse the fig leaves with the sugar until finely ground and fragrant.

Whisk the egg yolks in a small bowl.

In a saucepan, combine the fig-sugar mixture with the milk and 1 cup (240 ml) of the cream. Heat over medium heat until steaming, but not boiling. Slowly add a ladle of hot milk mixture to the yolks, a little at a time, while whisking constantly to temper the eggs. Repeat this twice. After you have added three ladles full of the hot milk mixture to the egg yolks, add the warmed yolks to the saucepan with the rest of the milk. Cook over medium-low heat, stirring constantly with a wooden spoon or heatproof spatula. Continue cooking until the mixture thickens and coats the back of the spoon (or until it reaches 180°F / 82°C), 5 to 7 minutes. Be sure not to let it boil.

Strain through a fine-mesh sieve into a bowl set over an ice bath with the remaining 1 cup (240 ml) of cream. It's fine if a few bits of fig leaf slip through. Stir in a pinch of salt. Chill the custard until very cold—at least 4 hours or overnight.

Churn in your ice cream maker according to the manufacturer's instructions. Transfer to a container and freeze for several hours to firm up.

APRICOT ALMOND CAKE WITH LAVENDER

This lovely little everyday cake is a mash-up of two favorite recipes of mine: Deb Perelman's Lemon Yogurt Anything Cake and Yotam Ottolenghi's Almond Apricot Cake. I use the lemon yogurt cake as the base, but substitute finely ground almonds for some of the all-purpose flour, and also add lavender. I bake it in an 8-inch (20 cm) square metal baking pan. The apricots are halved and nestle closely together on top of the batter. Many people feel like adding lavender makes things taste like soap. With only a teaspoon in the batter, the flavor is subtle, and balances out with the almonds and apricots. You can use fresh or dried lavender here. I also sometimes make this cake with whole-grain flour. If you try that, you will definitely need to up the lavender. This cake pairs nicely with a dollop of yogurt, and makes a delightful breakfast treat.

This cake does have a tendency to brown quickly on the top, especially if you are using a convection oven. If it starts to get too brown for your liking, you can put foil over the top for the last 10 to 15 minutes of baking. It keeps wonderfully (even improves!) at room temperature or in the fridge. *Jenna*

MAKES ONE 8-INCH (20 CM) SQUARE CAKE

Butter for the cake pan

½ cup (120 ml) olive oil

1 cup (200 g) granulated sugar

2 large lemons

3 large eggs

½ teaspoon vanilla extract

1 cup (240 g) Creamy Homemade Yogurt (page 292) or your favorite store-bought organic brand

2 teaspoons baking powder

½ teaspoon kosher salt

1 cup (120 g) all-purpose flour

½ cup (56 g) finely ground almonds

1½ teaspoons fresh or dried lavender

8 to 10 very ripe apricots, halved

Icing

6 tablespoons (48 g) powdered sugar

1 tablespoon fresh lemon juice

Preheat the oven to 350°F (180°C). Butter an 8-inch (20 cm) square baking pan or a 9-inch (23 cm) round cake pan. Line with parchment.

In a large bowl, combine the oil and sugar. Grate the zest from both lemons over the mixture. Whisk in the eggs, vanilla, and yogurt. Sprinkle with the baking powder and salt and whisk. Stir in the flour, ground almonds, and lavender. Pour the mixture into the prepared pan. Arrange the apricots on top of the batter, any way you like.

Bake until a toothpick inserted comes out mostly clean, with a few moist crumbs attached, about 45 minutes, checking to make sure the top isn't getting too brown. If it is, cover it with foil.

Let cool completely on a wire rack.

Make the icing: Combine the powdered sugar and lemon juice in a small bowl. Drizzle over the cake.

MUSKMELON SALAD WITH CUCUMBERS, SHALLOTS, AND GARDEN HERBS

SERVES 4 TO 6

2 shallots or 1 small red onion, sliced super thin into rounds

Red wine vinegar

Salt

3 different kinds of muskmelon, such as Goddess, Sharlyn, Galia, Canary, or Piel De Sapo

1 Armenian cucumber or 1 peeled and seeded English cucumber, cut into ¼-inch (6 mm) half-moons on the bias

1 cup (30 g) Italian flat-leaf parsley leaves

½ cup (15 g) fresh mint leaves

¼ cup (7 g) fresh tarragon leaves

Extra-virgin olive oil, for drizzling

Optional garnish: Fermented Chile Flakes (page 164), Espelette, or other chile flakes

10 paper-thin slices of a salty sheep's cheese such as Manchego or Pecorino

There are so many kinds of muskmelons, each with their own unique flavor and texture. We encourage you to explore beyond the usual cantaloupe and honeydew next summer—you might be surprised by what you find. One of our favorites is the Sharlynn melon, a large, oblong variety with a floral, almost tropical flavor and a melt-in-your-mouth texture. Galia melon is another standout, offering a green firm-textured flesh and a sweet, honey-like fragrance. For this salad, choose two or three types of muskmelon that contrast in taste and texture, and finish with a drizzle of high-quality olive oil. A salty cheese, like thinly sliced Manchego, takes it over the top. *Amon*

In a small bowl, combine the shallots or red onion with a splash of red wine vinegar and a pinch of salt. Toss gently and let sit for at least 10 minutes to mellow the flavor.

Cut the melons in half, scoop out the seeds, and remove the rind. For a polished look, use a melon baller or cut the flesh into uniform wedges or cubes.

On a large platter, layer the melon pieces and cucumber slices. Scatter the fresh parsley, mint, and tarragon leaves over the top, distributing them evenly for a vibrant presentation.

Using tongs or a slotted spoon, remove the pickled shallots and arrange them over the salad (hold onto the pickling liquid). Drizzle the salad generously with olive oil and a touch of red pickling liquid. Sprinkle with a pinch of salt and, if desired, a dusting of fermented chile flakes or Espelette for a subtle kick. Top with the slices of cheese.

Serve immediately.

MELON VARIETIES AND THEIR QUALITIES

Melons are a summer staple on the farm, and one of the most popular crops we grow. Whether eaten fresh, tossed into salads, or blended into drinks, these varieties add a delightful pop of flavor to your seasonal dishes. Below are some of our favorite melons, each with its own unique flavor, texture, and personality.

CANARY

This vibrant yellow melon has a smooth, waxy skin and a sweet, honeyed flavor. The flesh is pale green to white, with a crisp texture. It's perfect for snacking or adding to fruit salads.

PIEL DE SAPO

Also known as Santa Claus melon, this Spanish variety features a thick, green skin with mottled spots, resembling a toad's skin. Inside, its pale green flesh is sweet, with a crisp, refreshing crunch.

SHARLYN

These melons have a unique orange to white flesh and a strong, sweet aroma that is slightly musky. The texture is firm with a silky finish, making it an excellent addition to fruit salads or eaten on its own (our favorite).

GODDESS

This is the fastest growing melon on the farm and man is it a good one. Its skin is thin and lightly netted, and the flavor is subtly sweet with a refreshing aftertaste. It's an ideal melon for lighter desserts or wrapped in prosciutto.

GALIA

A cross between a cantaloupe and a honeydew, Galia melons have a pale-yellow skin with greenish netting. The flesh is vibrant green, soft, and very sweet, with a perfume-like aroma that elevates any dish.

CHARENTAIS

A classic French melon with delicate gray/orange skin that sometimes cracks at the blossom end, and a deep-orange flesh that is very aromatic. Its flavor is rich and complex, with notes of honey and a subtle muskiness. Ideal for a breakfast half-melon or a cocktail garnish.

HA'OGEN

Ha'ogen melons are known for their amazing tropical aroma and flavor. Left on your counter they will instantly make your kitchen smell like a tropical paradise. Their thin, pale-yellow skin and pillowy green flesh make them a go-to for a crowd-pleasing snack. They have a very mild, honey-like flavor.

SNOW LEOPARD

A striking melon with white, speckled skin. The flesh is white with a smooth texture and a subtly sweet flavor. It's perfect for a refreshing summer snack or as a garnish.

ORCHID WATERMELON

This watermelon variety has a beautiful bright-orange flesh, giving it a unique twist on the classic watermelon. It is sweet and crisp with a unique watermelon flavor. Great for fruit salads or as a chilled snack.

CRIMSON SWEET WATERMELON

This larger watermelon variety is the iconic one you might remember from your childhood. It has a deep-red flesh and is known for its perfect balance of sweetness and crunch.

SWEET CORN FROM THE WOOD OVEN WITH HERB BUTTER

SERVES 4 TO 6

8 tablespoons (115 g) unsalted butter, at room temperature

1 tablespoon finely chopped fresh oregano

1 tablespoon finely chopped fresh sage

1 tablespoon fresh thyme

1 teaspoon kosher salt

¼ teaspoon chile flakes, plus more for garnish

6 ears sweet corn, husked

Sweet corn was one of the first things that my parents grew when they first started farming. When I was a child, they would go out at 2 a.m. with headlamps into the field and pick the corn, filling the back of a red Chevy LUV pickup truck to the brim. The whole family would cram into the front and drive the corn to the Palo Alto farmers' market where they were accurately able to claim it was the "freshest" corn at the market. To me nothing says summer like corn on the cob. To tell you the truth, we often eat corn on the cob raw, without cooking or any additions; it doesn't really *need* anything else. That said, adding salty butter and some herbs elevates it for farm dinners or that Fourth-of-July barbecue.

We love to use our wood-fired pizza oven to make this when we are cooking for a crowd or before we make pizza, but if you don't have a pizza oven don't worry! A regular barbeque or broiler works just as well! *Amon*

In a small bowl, mix the butter, oregano, sage, thyme, salt, and chile flakes until well combined. Set aside or refrigerate if making ahead. Allow it to come to room temperature before serving.

Preheat a wood-fired oven, barbeque, or an oven broiler to at least 500°F (260°C).

If using a pizza oven or broiler, place the corn on a sheet pan close to your heat source. If using a barbeque, place the corn directly on the grill grate. Roast, turning occasionally, until the kernels are golden and slightly charred, 5 to 10 minutes.

Remove the corn from the oven and immediately slather each ear with the herb butter while still hot. Allow the butter to melt into the kernels, coating them evenly.

For extra flair, sprinkle a pinch of chile flakes or additional fresh herbs over the top before serving.

RED AND YELLOW WATERMELON SALAD WITH PICKLED RED ONION AND FETA

SERVES 6 TO 8

½ small red onion, thinly sliced

3 tablespoons (45 ml) red wine vinegar, plus more to taste

1 teaspoon mustard seeds

Pinch of salt

1 mini red watermelon

1 Yellow Doll or Orchid watermelon

½ cup (75 g) crumbled feta cheese

2 tablespoons extra-virgin olive oil

1 cup (30 g) tender mint leaves, for garnish

This salad plays with balancing sweet and salty. Don't be afraid to use a strong flavored feta or other sheep or goat's milk cheese here. The mild and sugary watermelon will balance it out. We top with pickled red onions to add some acid and more color onto an already colorful plate. It can get juicy, so we often serve it as a first course on its own plate rather than as a side dish. It's the ultimate way to celebrate one of the best things we grow at the farm. *Amon*

Place the thinly sliced red onion in a small heatproof bowl. In a saucepan, combine the vinegar, mustard seeds, and salt. Heat gently until the vinegar starts to simmer. Pour the mixture over the onions and let sit for at least 15 minutes while preparing the rest of the salad.

Slice off the tops and bottoms of the watermelons down to the flesh to give you a stable side. Set the watermelons cut-side down on a cutting board. Starting at the top, put a sharp knife between the rind and the flesh and carefully cut from the top down to the bottom, effectively "peeling" the watermelons. Take care to not cut off too much of the flesh. Continue cutting the rind off all the way around the melons.

Cut the watermelons in half lengthwise and set cut-side down on the cutting board. Cut the melon halves lengthwise into three or four long triangular wedges by angling your knife toward the core. Then cut these wedges crosswise into ½-inch (1.3 cm) chunks. Arrange the triangle pieces on a large serving platter, mixing the red and yellow melons for contrast.

Drain the pickled red onion and scatter it over the melons. Sprinkle the crumbled feta over the top. Drizzle the olive oil and an extra splash of red wine vinegar from the onions over the salad.

Add whole, small mint leaves over the top for a fresh herbal finish. Serve immediately as a light, refreshing side dish or centerpiece for a summer meal.

HEIRLOOM TOMATO STACK WITH GRILLED EGGPLANT, FRESH MOZZARELLA, AND PICKLED RED ONIONS

When summer finally hits full on, this is what we love to eat. It combines many of summer's most iconic ingredients. We pick the biggest, most colorful heirloom tomatoes we can get our hands on, mixing Marvel Stripes, Cherokee Purples, and Green Zebras to make an eye-catching platter. For the cheese, we like super-soft, fresh mozzarella cheese—the kind that comes packed in brine at the store. *Amon*

SWAPS/SPINS: **If you don't use up all your tomatoes and you have some extra grilled eggplant, this also makes for a yummy breakfast with a fried egg on top.**

SERVES 4 TO 6

1 medium globe eggplant, sliced into rounds ½ inch (1.3 cm) thick

3 tablespoons (45 ml) extra-virgin olive oil, plus more for drizzling

Salt

3 heirloom tomatoes (different colors), sliced into rounds ¼ inch (6 mm) thick

Freshly ground black pepper

6 slices fresh mozzarella

½ cup (65 g) Pickled Red Onions (page 132)

12 to 15 small whole fresh basil leaves

2 tablespoons balsamic vinegar

Preheat a grill or grill pan to medium-high heat.

Lightly brush both sides of the eggplant slices with olive oil and sprinkle with salt. Grill until the eggplant is tender with distinct grill marks on both sides, 3 to 4 minutes per side. Remove from the heat and let cool.

Arrange the heirloom tomato slices on a paper towel to absorb any excess moisture. Sprinkle lightly with salt and pepper to enhance their natural flavor.

On a serving platter, create horizontal layers by stacking in the following order:

A slice of grilled eggplant
A slice of fresh mozzarella
A slice of heirloom tomato (alternate colors for visual appeal)
A few pickled red onion slices
A few basil leaves

Repeat this layering process three or four times, depending on the size of your eggplant and tomatoes.

Scatter fresh basil leaves over the stacks. Drizzle with balsamic vinegar and olive oil. Finish with a pinch of salt and freshly ground black pepper.

TOMATO VARIETIES AND THEIR QUALITIES

Our business partner Andrew has been in charge of growing the tomatoes on the farm for over 30 years. He approaches this monumental task with gusto and a curious mind—finding the best varieties for our shifting tastes and climate. We like to tease him that we aren't really sure that he actually enjoys eating them, but he certainly is passionate about growing the best of the best. For those of us that do enjoy tomatoes, here are some standouts:

LARGE TOMATOES (from left to right in the photo on page 114)

ROMA

The ultimate sauce tomato. Firm, meaty, and low in seeds and water, these cook down into rich, velvety sauces.

COSTOLUTO

A deeply ribbed Italian heirloom with intense, Old World tomato flavor. Great sliced raw or slow-roasted.

CAROLINA GOLD

A smooth, golden-yellow tomato with a mild, sweet taste. Holds up well in sandwiches and salads.

BRANDYWINE

A classic heirloom! Large, pinkish-red, and packed with that deep, rich heirloom flavor. Juicy and perfect for BLTs.

LEMON BOY

Bright yellow, tangy-sweet, and slightly citrusy. Adds a pop of color to summer dishes.

STRIPED GERMAN

Gorgeous, marbled flesh with red and yellow streaks. Incredibly sweet and perfect for slicing.

GOLD MEDAL

A Marvel Stripe–type tomato with a fruity, almost tropical flavor. Beautiful on a Caprese platter.

CHEROKEE PURPLE

Deep reddish-purple with a smoky sweetness. A farm favorite for its complexity and rich flavor.

HOT STREAK

A striking red-orange tomato with a burst of flavor. Great for fresh eating or roasting.

EARLY GIRL

One of the first tomatoes to ripen each season! Medium-size, deep red, and packed with bright, sweet flavor. A reliable favorite for fresh eating and sandwiches.

CHERRY TOMATOES (clockwise from top left in the photo on page 114)

SWEET CHELSEA

A super-sweet, bright-red cherry tomato with thin skin and a juicy bite.

SWEET TREAT

Deep red and packed with flavor, these have a perfect balance of sweetness and acidity.

GOLD SPARK

Small, golden, and bursting with sweetness. Great for fresh eating and colorful salads.

SUNCHOCOLA

A unique, chocolate-colored cherry with a rich, complex flavor and a hint of smokiness.

CHOCOLATE SPRINKLES

Deep brown with green stripes, these have a rich, earthy sweetness.

SUN LEMON

A bright yellow cherry with a tart-sweet balance that adds a citrusy kick to dishes.

SUN GARNET

A deep, reddish-brown cherry with a full-bodied, almost wine-like flavor.

CLEMENTINE

Larger, orange, and incredibly juicy. Like a burst of sunshine in every bite!

SWEETHEART

A bright-red grape tomato with firm texture and concentrated sweetness. Ideal for roasting.

BLUSH

Beautiful oblong cherries with a yellow-pink gradient and a sweet, fruity flavor.

SUN CITRON

Pale yellow with a super-sweet flavor and a crisp bite.

ROSITA

A rosy pink cherry with thin skin and an almost candy-like sweetness.

SWEET MILLION

A classic red cherry tomato that produces in huge clusters. Sweet, reliable, and easy to love.

SUNGOLD

By far the farm favorite. Bright tangerine-colored fruit that is best eaten straight out of the basket!

SUNGOLD GAZPACHO WITH CUCUMBER AND SWEET PEPPER GARNISH

This recipe is inspired by one from *Ad Hoc At Home* by Thomas Keller. It has become one of our favorites and one that we come back to year after year. For the cherry tomatoes, you can use any yellow one, but the Sungold is the undisputed king of cherry tomatoes. We have tried year after year to replace it with something easier to pick and seed that is less expensive, but at the end of the day we always come back to it. It's our most popular cherry tomato variety and with good reason. We use Armenian cucumbers for this dish. Technically a melon, they have a softer skin and so do not require peeling. *Amon*

SERVES 4 TO 6

2 pounds (900 g) Sungold cherry tomatoes

1 cup (240 ml) water

1 Armenian cucumber (about 6 ounces / 170 g), roughly chopped or 1 large English cucumber, seeded and peeled

½ small yellow onion, roughly chopped

1 Jimmy Nardello pepper or other sweet red pepper, roughly chopped

1 cup (240 ml) extra-virgin olive oil

1 tablespoon sherry vinegar or other good-quality vinegar

½ teaspoon Fermented Chile Powder (page 164) or mild chile flakes

Salt

For Serving

½ Armenian cucumber, neatly diced

1 Jimmy Nardello pepper, neatly diced

Extra-virgin olive oil, for drizzling

In a high-powered blender or food processor, combine the tomatoes, water, chopped cucumber, onion, and yellow pepper. Blend until very smooth.

Pour the blended mixture through a fine-mesh sieve into a large bowl, pressing it gently with a spatula to extract as much liquid as possible. Discard any solids left in the sieve.

Return the strained liquid to the blender. With the blender running on low, slowly drizzle in the olive oil to emulsify, creating a silky, smooth texture. Add the sherry vinegar, chile flakes, and salt to taste. Continue blending until fully combined.

Transfer the gazpacho to a large bowl or pitcher. Cover and refrigerate for at least 1 hour to allow the flavors to meld and the soup to chill thoroughly.

To serve: Ladle the chilled gazpacho into chilled bowls or glasses. Top each serving with a sprinkle of the diced cucumber and red Jimmy Nardello. Finish with a light drizzle of olive oil for a final touch of richness.

NOTES:

For the smoothest texture, straining through a fine-mesh sieve removes any pulp or seeds, creating an elegant gazpacho.

Armenian cucumbers are ideal for dishes like this because their thin skin and mild flavor shine without any bitterness.

ZUCCHINI TEA CAKE

MAKES ONE STANDARD 8½- BY 4½-INCH (20 BY 10 CM) LOAF

¾ cup (150 g) vegetable oil, plus more for the pan

2 cups (240 g) Frassinetto flour or all-purpose flour, plus more for the pan

2 cups (290 g) grated zucchini

1 cup (200 g) sugar

3 large eggs (150 g total)

1 teaspoon vanilla extract

Zest of 1 lemon

¾ teaspoon baking powder

½ teaspoon baking soda

1 teaspoon ground cinnamon

½ teaspoon kosher salt

¼ teaspoon ground ginger

¼ teaspoon ground nutmeg

Zucchini is famous for its abundance. For many years, we have continued to cut back on how much we grow, and yet we always seem to have too much. We can't keep up with it, and inevitably some of it gets too big or we can't sell it all. It's exciting when it starts, and then after about a week there are only two ways to really enjoy eating it: calabacitas, in which it gets sautéed up with corn and beans and smothered in New Mexico green chile and cheese, or this zucchini tea cake. All of our tea cakes are whole-grain, made with Frassinetto or Rouge de Bordeaux flour that we grow and grind ourselves. The whole grains add a lot to the flavor and texture, and I highly recommend seeking out a local, whole-grain flour for this simple cake. *Jenna*

Preheat the oven to 325°F (160°C). Grease the loaf pan and dust with flour.

Put the zucchini in a sieve and press to remove excess moisture.

In a large bowl, whisk together the sugar, oil, eggs, vanilla, and lemon zest until smooth and well combined. In a separate bowl, sift together the flour, baking powder, baking soda, cinnamon, salt, ginger, and nutmeg. Gradually fold the dry ingredients into the wet mixture until just incorporated. Add the grated zucchini and mix gently to combine, being careful not to overmix.

Bake until a toothpick inserted into the center comes out clean, about 45 minutes.

Let the cake cool in the pan for 10 minutes, then transfer it to a wire rack to cool completely before slicing and serving.

STONE FRUIT CRISP

Use any combination of stone fruit for this crisp. I like including some plums for color but really you can use anything that is most flavorful: nectarines, peaches, apricots, etc. will all do the job here. I dislike the taste of cornstarch, so I usually use flour in the filling instead, knowing that the end result will be juicier than the cornstarch version. If you prefer a more jelled consistency in the final dish, feel free to sub cornstarch for the flour. You are looking for very ripe, soft fruit. This will allow you to cut down on sugar, which in turn will allow you to eat this for breakfast with yogurt in addition to vanilla ice cream for dessert. *Jenna*

SERVES 8

Softened unsalted butter, for the baking dish

Topping

1 cup (100 g) rolled oats

⅓ cup (40 g) all-purpose or whole wheat flour

⅓ cup (70 g) packed light brown sugar

½ teaspoon kosher salt

8 tablespoons (115 g) cold unsalted butter

Filling

8 cups (1.9 L) stone fruit, cut into ½-inch (1.3 cm) pieces, from about 9 pounds (4 kg) fruit, a single type or mixed

Juice of ½ lemon

1 cup (100 g) granulated sugar

2 tablespoons flour or cornstarch

Preheat the oven to 375°F (190°C). Butter a 2½-quart (2.5 L) or 9- by 11-inch (23 by 28 cm) glass baking dish.

Make the topping: In a food processor, combine the oats, flour, brown sugar, and salt and pulse a few times to break up the oats and combine everything well. Pour the mixture into a bowl. (If you do not have a food processor, skip this step and combine everything well with your fingers in a bowl.) Cut the butter over the top of the oat mixture and work the butter in with your fingers until evenly distributed. Set aside.

Make the filling: In a separate bowl, combine the fruit, lemon juice, granulated sugar, and flour and toss to coat.

Add the filling to the buttered baking dish. Sprinkle the topping over the top. Bake until the sides are bubbling and the filling has thickened, 30 to 35 minutes. Keep an eye on it while it is in the oven, and if the top is browning too quickly, place a sheet of foil loosely over the top. This will be extremely hot coming out of the oven. Place on a cooling rack and let cool. It's delicious warm, and can also be eaten at room temperature.

A BLACKBERRY PIE FOR PAUL

The legend goes that Amon's mom, Dru, wooed his dad, Paul, with a blackberry pie. She was running the student farm at UC Davis. He had left UC Berkeley with ambitions to start farming and was hired to advise at the student farm. I don't know whether his deep love of blackberries predated Dru's homemade pie, but that gesture of young love certainly solidified this sweet summer treat in Paul's heart. To this day, this is always what he asks for on his birthday. A friend gave us a few thornless blackberry plants several years ago, and although they struggle with our hot, dry summers, we can coax enough plump blackberries off of them to make a pie for Paul on his birthday.

I make this pie like my grandmother made her blueberry pies. I toss the berries in just enough flour to coat them. I cook roughly two-thirds of the berries with lemon and sugar, stirring frequently to avoid burning. Once most of the water has been cooked off, and the berries are thick and syrupy, I stir in the last third of the berries off the heat. I let this mixture cool in the fridge to evaporate some more moisture, and then pour it into my pie shell and bake.

I usually serve this pie very cold because 1) who wants to eat hot pie in 100°F weather and 2) since I don't add any cornstarch, it doesn't set up all that well. It is a soupier version than most, but once you add the ice cream or whipped cream to it, you won't mind a little extra blackberry syrup on your plate. *Jenna*

MAKES ONE 9-INCH (23 CM) PIE

6 cups (750 g) ripe blackberries

⅔ cup (150 g) sugar, or to taste

3 tablespoons (23 g) all-purpose flour

1 tablespoon lemon juice

1 recipe Pie Dough (page 294), chilled as directed

2 tablespoons butter

Preheat the oven to 350°F (180°C).

In a nonreactive bowl, combine two-thirds of the berries with the sugar, flour, and lemon juice and toss to coat. Transfer to a heavy-bottomed saucepan and cook them over medium heat, stirring frequently, until the juices start to thicken, about 10 minutes.

Remove from the heat and add the remaining berries. Put this mixture in the fridge, uncovered, until chilled (this will help evaporate some additional moisture and also keep your pie crust from melting). Chill for at least 4 hours.

continued

A Blackberry Pie for Paul, continued

When you are ready to bake the pie, roll out one disc of pie dough according to the instructions on page 294. Place it in a 9-inch (23 cm) pie pan and let the edges hang over the pie pan. Roll out the second disc of dough, and at this point you can cut decorative shapes or just make a few cuts to release the steam as the pie cooks. Add the blackberries to the pie shell, dot with the butter, and lay the top crust over the top. Trim the edges a bit and crimp the bottom and top crust together with your fingers or a fork.

Important! Put the pie pan on a sheet pan to catch any juices that sputter out. This is a juicy pie and it's going to be a hassle to clean the drips from the bottom of your oven.

Bake until you can see the juices bubbling, about 40 minutes.

Let cool to room temperature on a wire rack or chill in the fridge.

The Art of Being a Good Neighbor

When I lived in San Francisco, I had many neighbors. I knew none of them. My time outside of work was spent primarily with people just like me: busy young professionals, running from work to the gym and back to work. When I moved to the farm, one of my big concerns was whether I would make any friends or have any sort of social life.

The Capay Valley, where the farm is, is an interesting place demographically. During the 2016 election, I was speaking with a polling station employee who said that votes cast were split exactly evenly between Clinton and Trump: 100 votes for each. There are many families who have been here for generations, and many families who are newer transplants to the area. Perhaps "many" is a stretch, since there are only about four thousand people in the eighteen-mile ribbon of highway that makes up the Valley. There are a surprising number of organic and conventional farms, some that began in the 1980s and others that were started more recently by younger farmers with their small children, and not much other employment. Some folks commute to Bay Area cities for work. We also have a federally recognized tribe here that is an active and important part of the community. It is quite a diverse place, in all kinds of ways.

Little did I know that when I moved to the Valley, my friend group was about to expand significantly, in all directions. The thing I learned about living in a small place is there is a lovely interdependence that comes along with rural living. We borrow each other's equipment, watch each other's kids, cook meals when there is an illness or a death in the family or a new baby is born, and keep an eye out for dogs who have wandered too far from home.

This interdependence was on full display during the fires of 2020. As the LNU Complex Fire ripped across our hills, our local fire department learned that the state was not able to send any air or engine support for the Valley, given that most of California was also on fire. That left our local team of volunteers who, for thirty-six hours, went from property to property fighting the mighty blaze. Anyone with a tractor was out there, too, disking around homes and bringing water tanks.

While Amon (who is a captain for the Rumsey Fire Station) was out fighting the fire, I was at home with the three kids, wondering if and when I should leave. I had packed up the car with our important documents, my espresso machine, and some clothes (the espresso machine got packed up first, in case you were wondering about my priorities). In the middle of the night with the flames feeling a little too close for comfort, I took everyone down to Dru's house, which felt a little farther away and a little safer, and we stood outside as the kids slept peacefully in the safety of their grandmother's home. We watched in awe as the fire ate its way across the hills. At 1:00 a.m. I got a call from one of my dearest friends, who needed help getting her horses out as the fire was headed toward her home and six horses needed moving. When I arrived, there were already two other friends there to help her, and we could feel the heat from the flames as we loaded the horses into the trailers and took them to Full Belly for the night.

While the fires of 2020 are a good example of how we jump in to help each other when help is needed, life here is full of small acts of kindness and people acting out their values. A ride to town to pick up a car that is in the shop. Groups that gather to make quilts or sing together. Offering to teach a class to the kids who call this little valley home. Our Fourth-of-July parade, which we have dubbed The World's Tiniest Parade. Living in a small place requires good behavior. There is no anonymity here. When you live in a place where ongoing interdependence and interaction are a certainty, you are encouraged to be your best self. It's one of the things I most appreciate about living here. ***Jenna***

CORN AND SWEET PEPPER PIZZA

This summery pizza is a celebration of peak-season produce. Sweet corn and roasted Jimmy Nardello peppers are combined with garlic and fresh herbs for a light, flavorful pie. A squeeze of lemon and a sprinkle of parsley add brightness. *Amon*

SWAPS/SPINS: **If you have any pre-cooked corn or peppers from another dish, save them for this pizza! For extra depth, grill the corn and peppers before adding them to the pizza. If Jimmy Nardello peppers aren't available, substitute another sweet red pepper variety.**

SERVES 2 TO 4

2 balls Pizza Dough (page 297), at room temperature, stretched and ready for toppings

Flour, for dusting

Extra-virgin olive oil, for brushing

1 clove garlic, minced

2 Jimmy Nardello peppers, or other sweet red pepper, sliced into thin rings

1 ear sweet corn, kernels removed

8 ounces (225 g) mozzarella cheese, cubed or shredded (about 2 cups)

Fresh basil leaves, for topping

Grated lemon zest, for garnish

Chopped fresh parsley, for garnish

Preheat the oven or grill with a pizza stone to 500°F (260°C). Allow at least 30 minutes for the stone to heat fully. (Or use a pizza oven if you have one.)

Working with one pizza at a time, place the dough on a floured pizza peel or sheet pan. Brush the dough lightly with olive oil. Scatter half of the minced garlic evenly over the surface.

Arrange half of the Jimmy Nardello peppers over the dough, leaving space so you can see the crust! (When we prep our pizza team for pizza nights, we are always telling them less is more!) Sprinkle half the corn kernels evenly over the vegetables. Add a sparse layer of mozzarella.

Transfer the pizza to the pizza stone (or pizza oven) and bake until the cheese is bubbling and beginning to brown, the crust is golden, and the vegetables are slightly roasted, 7 to 10 minutes (or less in a pizza oven).

Remove the pizza from the oven and immediately top with fresh basil leaves. Sprinkle lemon zest and chopped parsley over the pizza. Slice and serve the pizza immediately!

Repeat with the second pizza.

NOTE:

As with any of our pizzas, less is more! You don't want to load down the dough with too many toppings, otherwise your crust will be a soggy mess with all the water releasing from the vegetables as they cook in the oven.

ROASTED JAPANESE EGGPLANT SALAD WITH HERBS AND LEMON-TAHINI YOGURT

SERVES 6 TO 8 AS A SIDE

2½ pounds (about 1.1 kg) Japanese or Chinese eggplants (3 to 4 medium)

2 tablespoons extra-virgin olive oil

1 teaspoon kosher salt

Marinade

½ cup (120 ml) olive oil

¼ cup (60 ml) fresh lemon juice

1 mild red chile, halved and seeded

1 cup (30 g) Italian flat-leaf parsley leaves

¼ cup (7 g) fresh mint or cilantro leaves

2 tablespoons fresh oregano leaves

6 cloves garlic, peeled

Lemon-Tahini Yogurt

½ cup (120 g) Creamy Homemade Yogurt (page 292) or your favorite store-bought organic brand

2 tablespoons tahini

1 teaspoon grated lemon zest

Pinch of salt

Eggplant comes in many different shapes and sizes and is cooked throughout the world in many amazing ways. One of my favorite varieties is the long and sleek black Japanese eggplant, which has few seeds, is firm, and has great texture when cooked. You can substitute any other kind of eggplant, but try to choose smaller ones so that every bite has some skin attached to hold it together. This recipe is adapted from the amazing *Ottolenghi* cookbook and is one of our more popular dishes at farm dinners. This dish will win over even people who are skeptical of eggplant. *Amon*

Preheat the oven to 425°F (220°C) using the convection setting if you have it.

Lay an eggplant (see Note) on a cutting board and make a diagonal cut crosswise at the blossom end. Roll the eggplant 20 to 30 degrees forward and make another diagonal cut 2 to 3 inches (5 to 7.5 cm) up to make a triangular piece. Continue rolling and cutting until you get to the stem. If the eggplants are more than 2 inches (5 cm) in diameter, cut them lengthwise before roll-cutting. You should end up with pieces that look like misshapen triangles. The goal is to create lots of surface area to soak up the marinade.

Place the eggplant wedges in a large bowl and toss them with the olive oil and salt. Arrange the eggplant on one large or two small sheet pans, with the cut-sides up and spaced apart so they are just barely touching but not overlapping. Transfer to the oven.

Roast until the eggplant turns golden brown, 15 to 20 minutes. Check the large pieces for doneness by pressing down on one—it should be soft all the way through. If your oven does not have a convection setting, this may take a bit longer.

Meanwhile, make the marinade: In a food processor, combine the olive oil, lemon juice, chile, parsley, mint, oregano, and garlic and pulse until the herbs are roughly chopped and the garlic is in tiny pieces. Resist the urge to blend into a smooth sauce—it's best with some texture.

Once the eggplant is done, remove it from the oven and immediately spoon about three-quarters of the marinade onto the eggplant. Make sure each piece gets a small coating of marinade. Let the eggplant marinate on the sheet pan as it cools to room temperature.

Make the tahini yogurt: In a small bowl, combine the yogurt, tahini, lemon zest, and salt and mix well.

When ready to serve, carefully transfer the eggplant and any marinade bits to a serving platter. Spoon the rest of the marinade over the top and drizzle with the tahini yogurt. Serve immediately.

If preparing ahead, keep the marinated eggplant separate from the tahini and combine just before serving. This dish is especially delicious served room temperature.

NOTE:

If you can only find globe or other round eggplant, cut into 2- to 3-inch (5 to 7.5 cm) misshapen cubes, making sure to leave a bit of skin on each piece to help it hold together.

CHERRY TOMATO PANZANELLA WITH PICKLED RED ONIONS

SERVES 6

5 cups (400 g) torn sourdough bread

½ cup (120 ml) olive oil

Salt

4 cups (600 g) mixed cherry tomatoes, halved

About 20 fresh basil leaves, plus more for garnish

½ cup (30 g) roughly chopped fresh Italian flat-leaf parsley

½ cup Pickled Red Onions (recipe follows)

5 cloves garlic, minced

2 tablespoons red onion pickling liquid

Freshly ground black pepper

This is one of our go-to dishes on a Monday in the summer after a farm event, when there are a couple of leftover loaves of bread. A crusty loaf that has started to go stale works best, but any high-quality sourdough bread will do. For the tomatoes, we love using a mix of colors and sizes. This simple salad is always a crowd-pleaser, and it's best enjoyed within 5 minutes of mixing everything together. *Jenna*

Preheat the oven to 375°F (190°C).

Tear the sourdough bread into bite-size chunks and place them on a sheet pan. Toss the bread with ¼ cup (60 ml) of the olive oil and ½ teaspoon salt. Bake until golden brown, about 10 minutes, turning the bread once or twice. Remove from the oven and let it cool for about 5 minutes.

Transfer the toasted bread to a large serving bowl. Add the halved cherry tomatoes, the remaining ¼ cup (60 ml) olive oil, basil, parsley, the pickled onions, garlic, and pickling liquid. Toss everything together and taste for salt. Adjust the seasoning as needed and finish with freshly ground black pepper. Toss once more, then garnish with additional basil. Serve immediately for the best flavor and texture.

PICKLED RED ONIONS OR SHALLOTS

MAKES ONE (8-OUNCE / 250 ML) JAR

1 small red onion or 6 shallots

1 cup (240 ml) red wine vinegar or rice vinegar

1 cup (240 ml) water

1 tablespoon sugar

1 teaspoon kosher salt

1 sprig fresh thyme

½ teaspoon coriander seeds

½ teaspoon yellow mustard seeds

Halve the onion through the root end, then slice it thinly to make half rounds. If using shallots, cut them into thin rings. In a bowl, combine the onions/shallots, vinegar, water, sugar, salt, thyme, coriander, and mustard seeds. Stir well and let sit for at least 5 minutes. These will keep in the refrigerator for up to a month, so make a double batch to add to other recipes and meals!